Ethics, Functionalism,
and Power in
International Politics

Other books by Kenneth W. Thompson

Ethics, Functionalism, and Power in International Politics

The Crisis in Values

Kenneth W. Thompson

Louisiana State University Press

Baton Rouge and London

Copyright © 1979 by Louisiana State University Press
All rights reserved
Manufactured in the United States of America

Design: Dwight Agner
Typeface: VIP Melior
Composition: The Composing Room of Michigan, Inc.
Printing: Thomson-Shore, Inc.
Binding: John H. Dekker & Sons, Inc.

1981 printing

LIBRARY OF CONGRESS CATALOGING IN PUBLICATION DATA

Thompson, Kenneth W   1921–
  Ethics, functionalism, and power in international
politics.

  Includes index.
  1. United States—Foreign relations—1945–
2. International relations.   3.   Political ethics.
I. Title.
JX1417.T48   327.73   78–24061
ISBN 0–8071–0492–2

TO OUR CHILDREN

Carolyn Annette
Kenneth Carlyle
Paul Andrew
James David

Contents

Preface

A handful of major approaches to international studies has for the past twenty-five years preoccupied Western scholars and observers whose resulting writings constitute the core of mid-twentieth-century international relations literature. Idealists and realists have contended with one another, and although their "great debate" was most intense in the 1950s and early 1960s, their differences are apparent in almost every controversy that has arisen over American foreign policy in the 1970s. Other main current approaches that have both unified and divided important groups of thinkers are functionalism, behaviorism, value theories, and decision-making. Taken together these perspectives deserve study and attention in the endeavor to assess international studies.

With the passage of the major American approaches to international problems into the last quarter-century, educators now point to the need both to analyze these contributions and assess their importance for the years ahead. New and old problems compete for attention on the foreign policy agenda. There is enough experience to make possible the testing of the relevance of an approach measured against the issues it is intended to illuminate. For some approaches, the zeal and enthusiasm with which they were first put forward can now be more judiciously expressed.

All this leads to an effort to deal somewhat more critically with the main currents of international thought. This book is intended to help students take a first step in that direction. Its scope is limited both by the size of the volume and the range of the author's knowledge, but it is at least a start. Because the debate over values is seen as fundamental to the culture's survival, the book begins with an inquiry into the crisis in values, examines the problems that arise in relating Christianity to politics, and goes on to reconsider idealism and realism. It selects for consideration an important approach to world order—functionalism—the principal architect of which was David Mitrany, a journalist, social historian, and political advisor to Lever Brothers.

The arguments that follow consider functionalism in relationship to higher education, the private foundations, and international agriculture. The test of functionalism, as with any approach, is its ability to bring some kind of order into a consideration of the social and international effects of particular forms of international cooperation. Finally, those who hold to a given approach have a duty to consider important problems in the light of such approaches. No issue has greater urgency for the republic today than the manner in which its leaders cope with change. Yet change can become a subject for serious study and discussion only within some sort of coherent framework. In other words, the approach we take to the problems of change are as vital as the facts of change itself.

There are numerous books dealing with the dominant approaches to international studies. This is a time, however, when someone should focus in depth on two or three such approaches as they relate to one another. It is the aim of this book to provide such a focus and open the way to a wider review by other writers.

I wish to thank Beverly Jarrett for her wise counsel, warm encouragement, and experienced editorial assistance. Preparation of the manuscript would not have been possible without the staunch support and patient help of two staff members of the Center for Advanced Studies at the University of Virginia, Frances Lackey and Maebelle Morris. In more than thirty years of scholarly effort, I have never worked with three more competent, considerate, and gracious colleagues.

Modified versions of some of the sections in this book have appeared in *British Journal of International Studies, Yearbook of World*

Affairs of the London Institute of World Affairs, Review of Politics, Virginia Quarterly Review, and in *American Thinking About Peace and War*, edited by Ken Booth and Moorhead Wright and published by the Harvester Press in Sussex, England.

Ethics, Functionalism,
and Power in
International Politics

I

The Problem of Values

Crisis in Values: Its Worldwide Dimensions

The crisis in values is more profound and all-pervasive than moralists and cynics alike acknowledge; it is also more far-reaching and worldwide than is commonly recognized or understood. This is a crisis which threatens not one but all four communities within which men live: the self; family and friends; the nation; and the globe.

Ironically, this widespread crisis has occurred simultaneously with an outpouring of social attention, compassion, and concern that is unparalleled in human history. Each of the four communities is the focus of an extraordinary amount of social concern. For the self, never before has society expended its resources so freely for promoting mental and public health among individuals and groups. There has never been more talk about seeking new means of holding families and friends together. The peoples of Asia and Africa, for whom national self-determination was long delayed, now share a status of equality in the United Nations with Russia and the United States. At the same time, the most urgent needs of mankind around the globe have been recognized at the World Food Conference, the World Environmental Conference, and the World Population Conference. Never before in the history of statecraft, declared Winston S. Churchill, has a nation displayed such magnanimity for others as the

United States showed for Europe in the assistance provided through the Marshall Plan.

Paradoxically, these advances in social and individual consciousness, which can be matched and multiplied in continuing struggles for civil and human rights, must be balanced against a decline in agreed-upon values among the same communities where progress is occurring. Twentieth century man's search for personal identity is so widespread and for many so desperate as to have earned Erik Erikson's designation as the identity crisis. On the level of interpersonal relations we speak of having become strangers to ourselves and those we love. Commonly accepted guidelines for living, as well as time-honored principles concerning life's origins and meaning, its sacredness and security, its preservation and termination, have been thrown into question or have broken down. To take life with premeditation was once universally a crime. Now there is a mixture of controversy, advocacy, and dissent about abortion, capital punishment, and mercy killings. Wars of national liberation and international police actions offer stark testimony that for the world community there are evidently values more precious than preservation of human life. A new California law invokes legislative authority to justify euthanasia when at least two doctors are agreed; and the beginnings of life are subject to medical intervention and to genetic engineering and a growing literature on the subject.

Looking out at the broad landscape of areas in which the sovereign individual yields to forces known and unknown that lie beyond his control, it is hard to escape the view that the deepest value crisis in modernity is the crisis of individualism. With the mushrooming of knowledge about the self, the individual grows anxious, unsure, beleaguered, troubled. An analogy with medicine suggests itself here. Throughout the summer months of 1976 I observed a group of skilled and experienced senior physicians and surgeons at work in a midwest hospital. What shocked me most as I watched them pondering next steps was their visible uncertainty about the best procedures when surgical patients were gravely ill. A friend at a great university medical school later explained that the explosion of medical knowledge has expanded the alternatives in diagnosis and

treatment exponentially for the physician. I had supposed that ignorance was the cause of the doctors' groping and searching for better
health care, but my medical friend informed me this was not the
case. Instead their greater knowledge had made them more aware of
complexities and unknowns. To name or identify a simple illness
had become the beginning, not the end of their work.

I would suggest that for individuals in society, dis-ease and anxiety may have similar roots. The self is an island in a vast turbulent
sea of contradictions and unknowns. It was assumed that as statistics
increased and knowledge multiplied, man's security would increase. Knowing thyself was rather too simply to be equated with
respecting thyself. Now we are discovering that the crisis of self
results less from lack of knowledge than from lack of a framework
within which to place that knowledge. What we are offered invariably is someone else's framework—Billy Graham's, Alex Comfort's,
Walter Cronkite's—with few of the assumptions spelled out. Or, in
the postmodern cultural era, beginning in the late sixties, we are
offered no framework at all. Part of our problem is that the demoli-
tion work has occurred with such lightning rapidity that we scarcely
know it has taken place or that we have accepted the change. Politics
is no exception.

One of my favorite political commentators is Sander Vanocur,
television columnist of the Washington *Post*. During the 1976 presidential campaign, Vanocur who subsequently joined the staff of the
American Broadcasting Corporation wrote:

> Television is going to miss this campaign. This campaign
> *was* television. Those wonderful people in *Common Cause*,
> who helped bring about limitations in presidential campaign
> spending, insured that in the 1976 race the medium would be
> the machine.
>
> If you felt something was missing in this campaign, if you
> looked for the buttons, the bumper stickers, the billboards and
> other forms of political graffiti that we had come to associate
> with past presidential campaigns, you could not find them. Too
> expensive. Save the money for the media.
>
> What you found instead were varying forms of media graffiti,
> especially on television, carefully packaged—whether paid-

3

political commercials or snippets on the evening news—and
designed to fertilize the hard soil of a political landscape
which, over the past decade, has yielded such a sorry crop.

If it has not, how could the presidential "debates" have assumed an importance far out of proportion to their substantive
significance? What used to count in presidential campaigns
was political muscle—organization, canvassing phone banks.
Now, in the age of the medium as the machine, the League of
Women Voters has become our precinct captain.

I think this is a burden that television is not equipped to bear.
The political process is too complicated, at times even too mys-
tical an experience for a medium that is designed, perhaps
unwittingly, to make brief claims on our attention spans.

We have heard from the pundits in the press and on television that it has been a lackluster campaign, devoid of any issues. But who is responsible? It is not the candidates. They
would be fools if they tried to explore issues in a medium that
measures out the world in 30-second takes. The medium is not
responsible.

. . . .

In an age where the medium has become the political process, it sets the stage, assigns all the roles and tells us when we
should laugh and when we should cry. It has become our Greek
chorus, mocking any attempts at reasoned political discourse.

It wasn't supposed to work out that way. But it has. And, God
help us, we seem to have accepted it.[1]

We live in a world free of basic premises and commitments or one
in which thinking and action is predicated on somebody else's
framework—a framework we are free to accept but seldom to assess
or reexamine.

If thinking about the self is in flux, thought about family and
friends is in a state of turmoil. Recent essays on friends and lovers
point out that distinctions the ancients made between the two are
conspicuously missing from our literature. Because we know some
things about some aspects of relations between partners, we assume
we know everything. What began as symbolic portrayal of human
relations is viewed today as the sum total of those relations. Adver-
tising men tell us that "how to do it" manuals will erase the tensions

4

and misunderstandings that have plagued this most intimate community of mankind's existence. Yet a wise Asian diplomat and cultural historian, former Indonesian Ambassador to the United States, Soedjatmoko, has asked how many husbands and wives ever comprehend the other's deepest thoughts and emotions. Even in those areas in which we claim to have abolished fear and ignorance, how far have we gone, how fragmentary is our knowledge? The National Endowment for the Humanities was asked to consider a proposal for commissioning movie scripts written by women, not men, on themes that presume to tell us what earlier generations were not free to view or discuss. I do not know in detail what was decided about the proposal, but a male review committee's first reaction apparently was that existing scripts written by males carried, in the words of the New York *Times*, "all the news that is fit [or necessary] to print."

The crisis of values within national communities is no less filled with poignant contradictions and inconsistencies. No sector is so evidently in midpassage regarding regnant ideologies. Crowded gas lines and wheat rust or nuclear pollution blown across national frontiers warn that the nation-state may be obsolete or dead. Bargains that provide short-run diplomatic gains in exchange for large-scale transfers of nuclear plant capacity lead potentially to proliferation of the most lethal weapons of war. Life-styles and transportation patterns in the industrialized states face drastic and far-reaching changes, because of new pricing structures and embargoes on oil today and other scarce raw materials tomorrow. The pound drops alarmingly in the nation-state with perhaps the greatest amount of foreign policy sophistication in the world.

At the same time, we hesitate and falter when asked to say what can take the place of nationalism. Transnationalism appears to have supplanted world government as the barely realizable goal of enlightened liberals. Yet newly independent nations take as much pride in national autonomy and crusading nationalism as Western states displayed a generation or two ago. The United Nations is at best a meeting place or forum for reconciling persistent national rivalries, not burying them once and for all for worldwide goals. The middle class in most industrialized states—particularly the up-

wardly mobile once lower classes of labor, blue collar workers, and
white ethnics—we are told, have become the archnationalists who
respond to the call that their nation be first, especially in defense.
Here we have the obverse of the displacement of the middle class in
Weimar Germany; an economically more favored class in the United
States that has climbed significantly up the economic ladder (though
not enough, according to its ambitions) now opposes multinational
corporations, any weakening of our defense systems, and even the
slightest diminution of national power and privilege. One need only
ask what we heard in the 1976 presidential campaign from two com-
paratively internationalist candidates about the United Nations, and
less-developed countries, or private initiatives abroad, to appreciate
the weight of such nationalist thinking.

The worldwide crisis in values partakes of some of the same
radical shifts, contradictions, and changes experienced in other
communities. Scholars returning to African countries after studying
in Europe and America experience it in such commonplace ways as
having to adjust from dining at high table to eating on the floor of an
African hut, or to serving in a university far more dependent on the
government. Their national leaders have come to power on the ex-
pectation that they will overturn the status quo and end subservience and deprivation. But what are the outlines and prospects of
change? What is desirable, necessary, and possible? A cacophony of
voices, each demanding and preempting the answers, competes to
be heard. Until recently prescriptions for change were being written
outside the third world. The list included population control, environmental programs, capital development, and technology transfer. To this list Africans juxtaposed as more urgent needs clean
water, national development, indigenous entrepreneurs, and intermediate technologies more appropriate to labor-intensive econo-
mies. Outsiders speak of raising annual per capita incomes dramatically, but World Bank reports place most of the poorer countries in the $50–$100 category. And if modernization necessitates
the destruction of cultural traditions permeating every facet of a poor
country's life, what will be the price and the damage in social disor-
ganization?

The Problem
of Values

I am convinced that the crisis in values is severe and apparently insoluble because, as the late Hannah Arendt put it, we are reluctant to talk about it. Talk is cheap, we say; what we need is policy and action. When men of affairs say a proposal is academic or merely theoretical, they are generally saying they can do without it. Sometime in the 1930s, Stephen Spender maintains, we entered the postmodern era—although in art and culture the Dadaists were forerunners of the era. Until then society, whatever its doubts about accepted standards, imagined that there was a tension between the traditional, the religious, the cultural and its art, politics, and prevailing values. My parents' generation, as I remember it, never imagined that the alternation and the loosening up of values after World War I was more than a temporary phenomenon. When you compare the atmosphere then with the shifts that have taken place in the last decade, the differences are all too apparent. In art and politics it seems that anything goes, and the standards against which to measure works of art and political actions are immediate satisfaction, personal gratification, and selfish gain.

If there is a way out of the present impasse—and no one reading history can be sanguine that historical trends are easily reversed—it is visible along the lines marked out by three propositions: 1) We need to rediscover and school ourselves in the ancient tradition of moral reasoning; 2) Whatever our satisfaction with general principles and truths, we should understand that values become powerful only in context; and 3) Where higher truths are involved, it is in their ordering character that they serve mankind, in their placing of the practical and immediate in tension with the ideal always lying beyond human reach. Each proposition deserves attention—more than can be offered here. Each proceeds on assumptions that demand inquiry and elaboration. Yet all have been abandoned by most pundits and political/educational leaders in our day. To elaborate each proposition:

1) Moral and political reasoning is certainly not the prevailing strategy for coping with present problems. Instead we prefer numbers from our leaders—growth rates and unemployment rates, test

scores and enrollments, miles per hour and gas consumption rates, numbers of bureaucrats and agencies, tax rates and income levels, percentages of voters voting and of women regularly achieving sexual gratification. Whatever we call this approach and however we line up on being precise or philosophical, this is plainly not moral reasoning. Moral reasoning assumes that clarification of values and their relation to one another is more important than plebiscites, majorities, or ideologies. It sees moral choice as the balancing of rights against rights, of antinomies before clearcut alternatives, of talking about problems when there is no copybook or final answer. The good competes with the good. We struggle with moral choice in every facet of our personal lives: loyalty to parents versus personal independence, being a good parent versus success in professional advancement, education for living versus the accumulation of high grades. On the national and international front, the clash is not less apparent: freedom of speech is in tension with the restraint of crying "fire" in a crowded theater; freedom of assembly for American Nazi party leaders may in some areas of Chicago threaten public safety and order, though that issue is still being debated vigorously by civil rights and public order groups as this goes to press. Extend this into the realm of political ethics about which President O. D. Corpuz of the University of the Philippines wrote in a memorable paper on the "Two Faces of Philippine Morality." Charged with extortion and having channeled public funds to relatives, former President Carlos Garcia justified his action by saying he had two loyalties: one to his family and compadres, the other to the state; and when the two were in conflict the former would win out.

2) Values almost never receive their power from scholarly treatises or reports on national goals by prestigious commissions. Their authority rests on their being identified and raised up from the tradition in reponse to urgent crises: the Declaration of Independence, the Emancipation Proclamation, Lincoln's letter to Horace Greeley, and perhaps the Four Freedoms. It is not only a matter of actions speaking louder than words. It is the words' being seen and understood as dwelling among us. Values are brought to bear on subject matter only when interpreted in context, as with love translated

into practice and justice undertaking to give each man his due as a relevant political ethic.

3) Finally, ideals and values need to be seen as standards beyond our grasp, but with which all our fragmentary strivings are in tension. This is a religious concept but, in the higher law tradition of the American constitutional system, no less a political idea. Part of our difficulty with values results from our reformist drive to translate and apply ultimate principles into practical programs for individuals and groups. We cling to the notion spurred on by commercialism, the weakening of religion, and a predominantly success ethic that nothing which won't fly is worth having or believing in. Yet there would be no Bill of Rights without the higher law tradition and no law without moral principles. Values have their roots and their history, time and season, transience and enduring truth. Unless we talk more about them in context and see them as they interconnect, arrange them hierarchically and study them at home and abroad, we are unlikely to recover from the crisis we are experiencing in values.

Politics and
Christianity*

We will hear much throughout the present campaign for president about religion and politics. Neither candidate is likely to say with the old-time Tammany boss, "For the life of me, I can't see what this God business has to do with practical politics." Both candidates and their families apparently are churchmen. Each speaks unashamedly of his own religious commitment.

It has not always been so. Religious people riding the crest of this latest wave of religious consciousness may forget that no Jew has become president, that no Catholic was elected until John F. Kennedy, and that even the majority group, the White Anglo Saxon Protestants, have, according to Gary Wills, lost credibility as the voice of America. What are the reasons that secular society is uneasy about

*Written during the 1976 campaign for president.

religion and politics? Why is there fear of the marriage of church and state?

Without accepting necessarily every item in the bill of particulars, my reading of the history of politics points up five major indictments leveled against those who claim they act from religion in politics. First, it is said that religion leads to hypocrisy because politicians seek moral justification for practical and selfish acts. In fact, the goal of politics is power, whereas that of religion is piety and virtue. A statesman is a dead or defeated politician, we are told. When he is faced with the choice of seeking the kingdom of heaven or seeking political office, it takes little imagination to know which comes first. Second, religion in politics generates self-righteousness and crusading zeal. Lincoln was a sad man, John F. Kennedy declared, because he found that in politics one can't have everything. In politics, Robert La Follette wrote, one must settle for half a loaf. Crusaders, whose grasp of what is righteous is all-encompassing, adapt less easily to the need for compromise. Third, religious men and women see the world as made up of "we and they"—Christians and barbarians, the saved and the damned. Politics is a world of coalition-building, strange bedfellows, temporary alliances however worthy their purposes. Fourth, for religion the knowledge of absolute right and wrong is seen as a practical possibility. There are the Ten Commandments, a code of ethics, a creed, and a doctrine. Politics proceeds on the basis of choosing the lesser evil, finding one's way in gray areas, making momentous choices with little certainty of the consequences. Fifth, religion, and in particular the great body of classical religion, was formulated in a time of sheep and shepherds attuned to pastoral life and shaped for a simpler, less complex existence. Life today is hurried and turbulent, shaken by crises in values, and divided by the clash of generations and cultures. Religion still concerns itself with the solitary individual whereas politics must organize and control large aggregates and groups, seeking through collective actions satisfactions that escape them in their personal lives.

Is it any wonder that skepticism is rampant and doubts multiply over whether religion has anything to say about politics? For those who doubt, it is not enough to recite answers to the five major indictments. It is not enough to say that hypocrisy is the tribute vice pays to virtue, that those who have found truth in ultimate terms will more readily compromise on proximate issues, that those who are saved will show compassion for the damned, that the great religions have never assumed earthly perfection in responding to strict moral codes, and that religious principles even though framed for a rural way of life are universal and true for all times and manners of living. Such answers are too general, self-confirming, and defensive to satisfy those who insist that religion and politics exist in two separate worlds and that the twain shall never meet.

So each of us in the end must find our own answers. The quest for what is right takes us down lonely paths dimly lit by any structure of thought. As a schoolboy, I struggled not with the theorems and principles of math but with the perplexities of combining and applying them. At the bedside of the dying patient neither euthanasia nor a commitment to the sanctity of life can guide the patient's family through choices directed primarily toward curbing the pain. So it is with religion, or, for me, Christianity and politics. Each of us must decide. Let me outline the four principles that for me serve to link Christianity and politics.

Life and politics are perceived fully and in depth when we recognize the tragic element and accept it as the groundwork of existence. Apart from Christianity and a few of the classics, where else does one turn for strength and illumination? Most popular teachers and preachers prepare us for life as a success story; politicians, depending on whether they belong to the ins or the outs, promise success yesterday, today, or tomorrow. But then who speaks of adversity, of dreams soured into illusions, of striving until death for ends that remain ever beyond our reach? Who tells of consequences and ills never anticipated, of panaceas that distract from more urgent tasks, of limits to human prescience, and of the arrogance of power rooted not in party or personalities but unchangingly in human frailty? Politicians can live for the day as myth-makers and image-builders, but only those with a tragic sense belong to the ages. Because the giants of Christian thought refuse to believe that the virtu-

11

ous are predestined to succeed in every earthly struggle, they help us to live with both triumph and tragedy in all dimensions of life, including the political dimension.

Further, Christianity helps me to live with ambiguity and the irrational. Every student of politics owes a debt to political rationalists from Plato to Walter Lippmann. The theory of politics would be barren of some of its profoundest insights without ancient and modern dialogues on the good life and the good state. Reason brings us to the threshold of political judgments concerning the good and the bad, the ideal and the better form of government, the best under the circumstances. Something more than pure reason, however, is needed when we cross the threshold into the realm of practical politics. Here moral and political judgment come into play. For here worthy purposes compete and conflict with one another. According to the Founding Fathers, a strong president and an effective Congress are necessary because although men in politics are good, men are also evil and thus in need of checks and balances. As devoted parents or responsible leaders we are never as virtuous as we claim to be. It is not only our perception that is limited, but also our will and our capacity to act beclouded by fears, insecurity, and, yes, by sin.

Then too the Christian in politics is obliged to live with the inevitable tension between ultimate and proximate levels of morality, holding fast to the one regardless of what may be required by the other. Love is the ultimate law of life, but political parties or leaders seldom love one another. Justice may be the highest expression of love in politics. Good fences and fair play make good political neighbors. Public and private morality may be in tension as exemplified in Lincoln's letter to Horace Greeley: "If I could preserve the Union and free all the slaves, I would do so; if I could preserve the Union and free some of the slaves I would do so; if I could preserve the Union and free none of the slaves I would do so. What I do, I do to preserve the Union." Yet public morality may also demand a higher expression of personal morality, for the leader must be purer than Caesar's wife, holding to both principles whatever the tension.

12

Finally, the political leader and the nation that would lead must offer their world not power alone but a moral example. Recently a leading journal, *Worldview*, inaugurated a moral audit of America's role in world politics—citing areas in which we advanced in our moral position in the world and areas in which we have fallen behind. For too long we have assumed that our military or economic balance sheet charted where we stood. All but forgotten is the fact that our influence has been greatest when others saw in us a promised land not a wasteland. Any one of us knows when we have been in the presence of moral greatness. Following forty-two days at the bedside of my ninety-five-year-old mother in the summer of 1976 as her life ebbed away, I knew myself to be in the presence of such greatness, and I wrote: "She praised God not by words but through the example of her life . . . [and] bequeathed lessons and truths good for a lifetime."

At some time in their lives, most men have known the force of moral example. The nation has known it in its great leaders. The world has seen it in our country's finest hours. And when we rise to these heights again others will praise us as we praise a good mother or father.

Idealism and Realism:
Beyond the Great Debate

The tendency of all debates is to exaggerate and to overkill, to claim and condemn too much. Then when the smoke has lifted and guns have been silenced, those who remain discover that the world is more complex and answers less certain than the debaters had led them to believe. It is as though worthy causes could not advance unless carried on the backs of overstatements. If we survey our own lifetime, we cannot fail to note the progress that has been made toward minority rights, women's liberation, the rights of the working man. Whenever movement has occurred, though, it has come in response to politics, propaganda, and pressures. It has come because someone with a credible, even noble cause planned and organized, but in their action almost always overdid at the price of generating reaction and counterattack. It may be stretching a point to compare thinking and political movements with wars; yet there is action and reaction, attack and counterattack in all three areas, reminding us of Sir Herbert Butterfield's words: "Many of us have been brought up on a kind of history which sees the human drama throughout the ages as a straight conflict between right and wrong. Sooner or later, however, we may find ourselves awakened to the fact that in a given war there have been virtuous and reasonable men earnestly fighting on both sides. Historians ultimately move to a higher altitude and produce a picture which has greater depth because it does justice to what was thought and felt by the better men in both parties."[2]

Butterfield is indeed on one side of our argument today; plainly he belongs to the political realists. His realism, however, is tempered by his profession as historian and by Britain's long tradition in foreign policy wherein power politics has come to be viewed as unremarkable. "In politics," he writes, "we may be partly responsible for one another's sins." For he sees at the core of international conflict a Hobbesian fear casting a fateful shadow over states. Nations joined in peaceful or not so peaceful competition are caught up in a profound moral predicament as in the Cold War:

> There could be a United States and a Russia standing at the top of the world, exactly equal in power, exactly equal in virtue; and each could fear with some justice that the other might steal a march on it, neither of them understanding for a moment—neither of them even crediting—the counterfear of the other. Each could be sure of its own good intentions, but might not trust the other, since one can never really pierce to the interior of anybody else. Mutual resentment would come to be doubted because, on the top of everything each party felt the other was withholding just the thing that would enable it to feel secure. This situation may never exist in its purity, but the essential predicament underlies international relations generally, making even simple problems sometimes insoluble.[3]

The moral predicament of which Butterfield speaks would be fateful enough if fear and anxiety were the preoccupation of individual leaders, of Henry Kissinger or Cyrus Vance and Andrei Gromyko and Gerald Ford or Jimmy Carter and Leonid Brezhnev. Its force is multiplied many thousand-fold by the fact that foreign policy is everyone's business and the fears of a secretary or foreign minister are magnified and intensified in the masses' unease and in the dreams and frustrations of the man in the street. In Butterfield's words: "The key to everything... lies in the mediocre desires, the intellectual confusions and the willful moods of the average man, the man in the street. The real trouble is the moderate cupidity of Everyman—his ordinary longing to advance a little further than his father, or simply to increase his sales—even just his dread of a decline in his standard of living. This, when multiplied by millions, can build up into a tremendous pressure on government."[4] It is precisely these fears that bring states to the brink of war. Each side pursues its security through power but "may overlook the fact that it can make its own security complete only by destroying the security of the other altogether."[5] The security/power dilemma is the most urgent problem of war and peace, and the great test of idealism and realism must be how fully they understand and how effectively they prepare Everyman and his leaders for coping with this dilemma.

1. IDEALISM Idealism looked primarily to international law and organization as the means through which the security-power dilemma among nation-states can be resolved. Leaving aside the numerous peace plans and grand designs proposed from Immanuel Kant to Woodrow Wilson, the first major steps in the long history of international organization came with the First and Second Hague Peace Conferences of 1899 and 1907. Writing in 1962, in his definitive history of the first conference, Professor Calvin D. Davis concludes: "The First Hague Peace Conference achieved little in the way of progress for humanity.... The conventions and declarations at The Hague in 1899 and later agreements based upon those documents were paper achievements, masks concealing failure."[6] Looking back after more than a decade, however, Davis found his own judgment too harsh, explaining that though the conference had not considered any of the prime political problems of the era, it had laid the foundations for new approaches to arms limitation, international arbitration, and the laws of war, especially the latter. The first con-

15

ference founded the Permanent Court of Arbitration with a list of names of arbiters and judges; the second conference drafted a convention for a world court, failing only to find the means of appointing judges, a failure that was resolved when the Permanent Court of International Justice was inaugurated on February 15, 1922. Of four American members of the Permanent Court of Arbitration, only one, John Bassett Moore, accepted election by the council and assembly of the League "notwithstanding that he had opposed American entry into the League."[7]

From the outset, it was fear of other nations and the high cost of armaments that inspired international initiatives. The decision to call the conference of 1899 originated within the Russian finance ministry, as Russia and Austria sought to avoid the strains of matching France and Germany in an artillery buildup. Leaders reacted with skepticism and sometimes with negativism. Lord Salisbury warned that arms were "a serious deterrent to war." The Prince of Wales suspected the Russian ministers of intrigue. Kaiser Wilhelm II privately warned his foreign minister, Count Bernhard von Bülow, that there could be a "bit of deviltry" in Russia's move. The French feared dire effects on their military position, and the United States telegraphed acceptance to participate but explained that the war with Spain made arms limitations below the present level impractical. Alfred T. Mahan pointed to Russian concern with American power as the probable motivating factor, and Rudyard Kipling wrote the poem, "The Bear that Walks Like a Man."

Nevertheless, the conference went forward in part because all questions concerning the political relations of states were excluded. Many points in the existing law of war had never received formal international sanction, and it was in this area that progress resulted. Yet enthusiasm in the United States, Britain, and France focused more on the possibility of permanent international conferences and arbitration than on armaments, perhaps because arbitration between the United States and Britain had occasionally been successful.

Writing of the Second Hague Conference, Davis notes that any student of international affairs "would have quickly decided that the appellation 'Peace Conference' meant little." Its main business was war and the laws of war. "Proposals for limiting armaments had failed even before the Second Hague Peace Conference opened." The leaders of every major power alternated between praising and scorning the conference. Theodore Roosevelt's movement from public enthusiasm to private disdain was typical. In all the notes and confidential talks in the year preceding the conference, "none believed that his government threatened his neighbors, yet each feared his country's neighbors."[8] It was this fear of threats by neighbor-states and not the novel methods or procedures at the Hague that determined the course of each nation's foreign policy and brought on World War I. The thousands of documents and millions of words that passed among statesmen had less value than would have a mutual recognition of the security/power dilemma in which the major powers were all caught up. Understanding would have been more important than organization.

Idealists are not oblivious to human nature or to the threat inherent in the security/power dilemma, but they put less stress on these factors than on laws and structures. They are more likely to see the world as made up of good and evil men, law-abiding and lawless men, and to assume that peace will be secure once the latter have been defeated. Political realists are more likely to throw the spotlight on the situation out of which evil men emerge and the circumstances that might lead to their return. "Men like Hitler do appear—tending to emerge, however, out of situations which have provided an unusual opening for them ... or tempted them to try to cut some Gordian knot." It is the same with armaments, because "the reason for arming is the predicament itself and it is wrong to insist that one is arming only because the other party is absolutely wicked, wrong to imagine that we on our side have the right to bigger weapons because we are arming Righteousness."[9]

This may be true, the idealists counter, under the present international system; but problems such as fear and insecurity will disappear under a new and better system. The two pillars of idealist thinking on the ground of which realists do battle are these: 1) that a new world order will be superior to the old, an assumption that prompted Carl Becker to ask in 1944 in the title of his book, *How New Will*

the Better World Be?, and 2) that laws and structures are capable
of transforming human nature. On the first, the realists speak essentially with one voice. With Sir Herbert Butterfield, they would
maintain:

> Like our forefathers, we may feel that the world was spoiled
> before ever we were born. We face systems of society not quite
> the same now as in feudal times, but such as have been defeat-
> ing the human race for centuries. It is pointless for us to blame
> our predecessors, for they handed down to us a world of
> patches and compromises, because they too had their desperate
> moments, wondering sometimes whether they could keep the
> world on its legs at all. In any case, a few million decent people
> like us with the normal amount of egotism, would tangle every-
> thing up within fifty years even if they had a clean start.[10]

The belief that new institutions are superior to the old has been true
of the United Nations. Secretary of State Cordell Hull in 1943 on his
return from the Moscow conference proclaimed that the new organization would mean the end of power politics and usher in a new era
of international collaboration.[11] The historian's skepticism about the
idealist claim stems from the knowledge applicable to almost every
organization—that it starts afresh but becomes tangled in all the old
forces.

The realist criticism of the second idealist tenet of faith, that
institutions change men, is more equivocal; for to the realists as to
the idealists, it must be obvious that certain laws and patterns of
society seem more capable of generating humanitarian responses. I
worked for twenty years for a large American foundation, and the
conduct of its officers was unmistakably influenced by its mandate
"to serve the well-being of mankind throughout the world." Lights
burning late at night in offices of top State Department officials,
especially when the secretary of state draws heavily upon human
resources in the department, are a testimony to the force of laboring under another noble banner, the quest for peace and national
security.

While acknowledging the influence of circumstances on individuals, the realist would say, "It is wrong to suppose that just the
pattern of society is the cause of selfishness in human beings." A

18

social order with checks and balances and machinery through which both creative and self-centered impulses may be constructively channeled can lead men to behave better than they otherwise would. "There is always more latent evil and more potentiality for aggressiveness than actually emerges in normal societies and in settled times." The realist would agree it is important to seek a more orderly international system, though the risk for the weak and the poor is that the system often reflects order as seen from the standpoint of the strong and the rich. Law and frequent international conferences serve as one instrument for bringing about change; politics and power represent another. In Butterfield's words:

> An international system acts [effectively] . . . when, by inhibition as well as prohibition, it operates to restrain a predominant power. Any state, once it sees that it can do what it likes with impunity, tends to move to aggressive policies, however virtuous it may hitherto have been. This has been confirmed in modern times when Spain, France, Germany, and Russia have successively emerged as "the menace to the European continent." The same has been true of small states when they have had a local opportunity.
>
> When, in the nineteenth century, it was held that Russia would become a terrible threat if ever she pulled herself together, the calculation was based on the ordinary operations of human nature in a country still officially Christian. One might have expected Communism to disdain such acquisitiveness, but no! It brings an additional motive for aggrandizement—the desire to spread a better order of society. The United States, having run to excess in its contempt for power politics, catches a parallel kind of missionary zeal, so that she is in danger of increasing the evil by her mode of combating it.[12]

What realists argue, in their criticism of the idealist crusade for a new and better world cast in the image of utopia's spokesman, is that such a course leads to running roughshod over so-called lawbreakers or revolutionary nationalists without seeking to understand their circumstances.

> The most subtle and unreachable problem of politics, and one of the profoundest seats of evil, is . . . self-righteousness, which sometimes produces more terrible results than *realpolitik*. It is

even a mistake if academic people—or liberals of a second
generation who have not really felt the toughness of the
world—take to painting their enemies as too vile in their wick-
edness or sincerely feel them to be. . . . And though the promotion of benevolent causes is an important thing, this does not
vindicate the kind of people who hate the capitalists more than
they love the poor. The essence of the fight between good and
evil is something that happens at a different level altogether
inside every one of us.[13]

2. REALISM The thoughts contained in this concluding sentence in
the realist criticism of idealism along with another sentence, "Too
easily one overlooks the amount that can be achieved by the kind of
thought that reconciles,"[14] lie at the heart of political realism. Because realism assumes that international politics, like all politics, is
engaged in by imperfect men and nations, it takes for granted compromise, give-and-take, and reconciliation. The watchword of diplomacy is accommodation; a political settlement is the most to be
hoped for among rival states. Reality, as Lincoln saw it, is too twisted
for any set doctrine. Dogmatism stands in the way of reconciliation.
John Milton wrote in his great treatise on freedom, *Areopagitica*:
"There be . . . who perpetually complain of schisms and sects, and
make it such a calamity that any man dissents from their maxims.
'Tis their own pride and ignorance which causes the disturbing, who
neither will hear with weakness, nor can convince, yet all must be
suppressed which is not found in their Syntagoma."[15]

Nor would the realists accept the idealists' charge that there is no
morality in hard-won compromise but only a cynical response to
power. The realists call forth a hero of idealism, Hugo Grotius, who
in the preface to *De Jure Bell ac Pacis (The Law of War and Peace)*
warned: "I saw prevailing through the Christian world a license in
making war of which even barbarous nations would have been
ashamed. Recourse was had to arms for slight reason or no reason;
and once arms were taken up, all respect for divine and human law
was thrown aside, as if men were thereafter authorized to commit all
crimes without restraint."[16] They remember John Bunyan's advice
in *Pilgrim's Progress* to Talkative: "The Soul of Religion is the

Pratick part,"[17] and on the issue of structure and organization the words of Benjamin Jowett: "The spirit creates the organization and the organization kills the spirit." To this the idealists offer their own strong response:

> The average man who expresses opinions on foreign policy appears to take it for granted that the conduct of governments in their external relations is a proper subject for moral judgment. He condemns governments, usually foreign, but sometimes even his own, for acts which he describes as immoral, unjust, wrong, evil, barbarous,and he commends government, usually his own but sometimes even foreign, for acts which he describes as good, just, upright.[18]

It is as impossible for men or nations to free themselves from moral judgments or estimates of right and wrong on foreign policy as it would be to shed their feelings over justice and injustice in their personal lives. Indeed this story is told of Attorney General Robert Kennedy's meeting with a group of religious leaders early in the Vietnam War. After explaining that national leaders had to weigh considerations from which private citizens might consider themselves immune, Kennedy encouraged his visitors to keep up their criticism, saying their views might force the government to be more moral and humane than "reasons of state" would otherwise lead them to be. Idealists also argue that even America's archrealists, such as Theodore Roosevelt and Alfred T. Mahan, never argued for divorcing foreign policy from ordinary decency and humanity. Roosevelt's relations, incidentally, in the year preceding the Second Hague Peace Conference, with the American Peace Society and other peace groups is a case in point, supportive perhaps of both idealists and realists. For Roosevelt agreed with the peace groups that the conference should go forward but warned that were the United States to disarm, as had been urged, we would be "at the mercy ... of other peoples still in the stage of military barbarism or military despotism."[19] He feared that a conference whose spokesmen failed to recognize the need for both arbitration and armaments would raise public expectations too high and lead to disillusionment, since governments were obliged to safeguard national security. It remained for another realist writing decades later, the theologian Reinhold Niebuhr, to draw a distinction between governments—whose first duty was to protect generations alive and yet unborn through following the national interest—and the people, whose duty was to press their governments to attend, in certain cases at least, to the needs of humanity at large. Percy Corbett affirmed this point in somewhat different language when he said that the state is nothing more than an instrument for human needs and well-being and should respond to the basic human aspiration to raise the moral level of national behavior. One such desire and aspiration is that of serving a world larger than the national group, of being useful to the basic needs of humanity at large. It is unrealistic, the idealists insist, to deny that certain worthy and worldwide goals are imposed on a government by its constituents who today are not only citizens of a nation, but, if their nation is to survive, citizens of the world. America's finest hours have been moments in which narrow nationalism has been transcended, as in the case of supporting the Marshall Plan.

The Marshall Plan, realists respond, is an example of the highest moral possibility of nations, but also an indicator of the factors that come into play in moral judgment. What made the policies that led to the Marshall Plan a practical possibility was the convergence of interests within and between nations. Within the United States and in particular in the Congress, churchmen and idealists who wished to see an alleviation of human suffering and wartime devastation in Europe joined hands with realists and militarists who argued that an enfeebled and war-torn Europe would constitute a political vacuum into which Russian influence and power was certain to spread. From the standpoint of the Atlantic community, Europe's inherent need for economic recovery and political stability merged with the American interest in resisting Soviet expansionism. International politics, as politics within national communities, is lived at the point of convergence of particular and universalistic interests. If this is something less than abstract love and justice, it is more than a totally self-centered narrow nationalism. Sometimes in politics, as in life, enlightened self-interest is man's highest moral attainment. At the groundwork of man's noblest endeavors the outside observer finds

22

a curious mixture of motives. I do what I do for my children out of love and devotion, but also that they may honor my name. Moreover, love of family left to itself may lead to a neglect of wider communities as in the case of former President Garcia of the Philippines who responded, as we have seen, that when loyalty to his state conflicted with loyalty to his "compadres," the latter must always take precedence.

Such conflicts of loyalty, the idealists answer, may once have controlled the acts of statesmen, but this was in the era of nationalism. Today we live in an interdependent world. Not only have thermonuclear weapons made war obsolete in the settlement of disputes among nations, but nations themselves are obsolete. Percy Corbett asks: "Have not science and technology made it finally clear that national power cannot ensure the attainment and preservation of those values that make life worth living." His answer is that there must be "an operative recognition of moral values transcending all particular State interests." Writing in 1956 Corbett warned that this change was not something that could be "brought about in a day or a year." Power remains an important element in politics, but "the ephemeral nature of any particular power constellation is one of the many reasons that makes it more practical wisdom for the United States to shift some of the emphasis in its foreign policy from the accumulation of national power to the promotion of supranational institutions designed to keep the competition for power from breaking out into war." [20]

In the end, the idealists rest their case against realism on essentially three propositions: 1) The ancient methods of controlling international conflict and preventing the outbreak of war, especially that of maintaining the balance of power, have not worked. 2) The disparagement of international law by those who write of the legalistic-moralistic approach to foreign policy obscures the importance of rules of conduct among nation-states. 3) Justice is a preeminent concern today among men and nations, and only those approaches that recognize this will stand the test of time. It is on these key points that the issue is joined by those who reject both the major assumptions and most important conclusions of political realism.

To the first proposition, the realists respond that the indictment is both true and false. The international system has broken down and war ensued tragically enough far too often for the thousands of dead and maimed who have been its victims. There have also been long periods of peace, as following the Congress of Vienna, when for almost a century the five major powers found themselves at war with one another for only a total of eighteen months. When aggressors or nations seeking to expand their influence have expected resistance from nations with equal or greater power, they have more often limited their ambitions and not turned to war. It is also fallacious, the realists say, to suppose that nothing has been learned about the causes and prevention of war in more than three hundred years of experience with the modern state system or more than two thousand years of experience with the world's great civilizations. There is, they say, an air of pretension in claiming that the model of the American federal system, for example, which has brought a nation of 100–200 million people relative peace and stability would do the same for 4 billion people in vastly different social, economic, and political circumstances. Moreover, the federal system, when it came into being, was proclaimed "a more perfect union," implying that the union already existed before the constitution. What was in existence was a community of shared values and experiences conspicuously lacking on the world scene. Finally, realists remind the enthusiasts for new approaches to peace who call for the abandonment of older approaches because of their failure to prevent wars that all the highly touted and elaborate machinery of present-day economics has not succeeded in preventing inflation, unemployment, and recessions in individual countries around the world.

To the second proposition the realists acknowledge that international law has often had, and may continue to have, a humanizing and civilizing influence among men and nations. They would agree with a great international jurist, Charles de Visscher, who wrote: "The international community is a potential order.... It does not correspond to an effectively established order. It falls short of a legal community in that it lacks legal control of the use force, which essentially implies three things: general adherence to the distinction

24

between the legal and illegal use of force, establishment of a system of peaceful change, and organized collective repression of aggression."[21] De Visscher and the realists would also agree that the separation of international law from its social, political, and moral circumstances was a mistake. "The distinction between ethical and legal categories, reasonable in itself and in many ways necessary, must not be pushed to the point of completely separating law from the primary moral notions." To pretend that men confined within close-knit national communities were likely to take a universal moral outlook was wrong, for in de Visscher's words: "Merely to invoke the idea of an international community, as the habit is, is immediately to move into a vicious circle, for it is to postulate in men, shut in their national compartments, something that they still largely lack, namely the community spirit, the deliberate adherence to supranational values."[22] From one other standpoint, de Visscher and the realists hold a common view articulated by him when he maintained: "The central problem of the normative order is henceforth much less the legal validity of the formal process of elaborating international law than the obstacles confronting its extension."[23]

While de Visscher, more than the idealists, was sensitive to the limitations of present-day international law, he pressed more forcefully than any of the realists for use of the International Court on which he sat and for the building of a network of international institutions that would serve the human person. Realists look with deep skepticism on the immense commitment of time and energy given to drafting international legal conventions and promoting the spread of principles of law when the resolution of conflict is more often determined by nonlegal means. They distrust the disproportionate influence of lawyers in shaping American foreign policy and criticize the tendency of lawyers to be defenders of the status quo. It would be far better, they feel, to examine the political and social situation that gives nations and their leaders an interest and a stake in observing legal undertakings than to laud formal legal arrangements that are often observed more in the breach than the keeping.

Finally, insofar as justice is concerned, realists insist that it consists of more than past legal conventions. The new nations of Asia

25

and Africa wish as often to change the law fashioned by the developed and industrialized Western nations as to observe it. Yet realists are also, with a few exceptions, prisoners of their culture. They judge the Third World, its influence and its power and the interests and values of its people, by Western standards and are frustrated and offended when they misunderstand and miscalculate. It is no accident that Secretary of State Kissinger, preeminently a realist, turned his attention to the problems of Africa only in the waning days of the Ford administration. A more profound realist, Reinhold Niebuhr recognized the Third World's importance much earlier, warning it was folly to pretend that the West's problems in relations with the developing world were the same as with other regions. He was among the first to warn "that both our system of democracy and our high standard of living seem irrelevant in Asia and Africa." [24]

It was not enough to say that exporting American know-how would bring these societies into the twentieth century, however benevolent the motives and the idealism behind such an effort. The industrial countries were not virtuous enough to sustain such an effort; nor would it be relevant if they did. Yet to counsel benign neglect or to turn against the Third World out of dismay and because of cultural differences was foreign to Niebuhr as well, not only because of his concern for justice, but because the influence and interests of these people will make international cooperation imperative both from the East and the West.

3. CONCLUSION The tragedy of the debate between idealism and realism exists because most of its critics and some of its spokesmen have confused the real issues. Both represent tendencies and broad outlooks; they offer few if any panaceas or instant solutions to policy problems. Too often the pride and the zeal of the debaters have pushed their proponents to frame their views in what became fateful choices, an either-or way of thinking. The wisest among them as, for example, Reinhold Niebuhr, recognized the interconnections of the two views. Writing in 1932 in *Moral Man and Immoral Society*, Niebuhr said, "Politics will, to the end of history, be an area where

conscience and power meet, where the ethical and coercive factors of human life will interpenetrate and work out their tentative and uneasy compromises."[25] In another earlier era, Blaise Pascal in *Pensées*, No. 416, wrote: "Justice without force is impotent, force without justice is tyrannical. It is necessary, therefore, to unite justice and force and to make that which is just strong and that which is strong just." We may be awaiting a new synthesis, an outlook that strives with more determination to combine the ideal and the real. Until then we can do worse than to listen to some of the wiser realists and the wiser idealists whose views have informed the substance of this critical review.

II Ethics in War and Peace

Questions of right and wrong, justice and injustice, good and evil, virtue and iniquity lie at the heart of political theory. Normative discussions are inescapable themes in all political discourse. It would be strange if ethics were excluded from debates over international problems, especially in the American republic whose founders spoke and wrote in the language of moral and political theory.

Americans have been inclined both to exaggerate the scope and overstate the limitations of ethical thinking on war and peace. Paradoxically, these two tendencies have often been expressed by the same leader or scholar. President Theodore Roosevelt, for example, in his early associations with Andrew Carnegie encouraged the most utopian dreams of that powerful industrialist. (It was Carnegie who instructed the trustees of the Carnegie Endowment for International Peace to direct their attention first to the elimination of war and, when this objective had been realized, to turn then to other urgent problems.) Yet it was also President Roosevelt who spoke of "speaking softly and carrying a big stick" and heaped scorn on those, including Carnegie, who when planning for the Second Hague Conference proposed that the United States reduce substantially its national defense capacity. General Douglas MacArthur was an outspoken champion of world government; yet he favored a military policy in Korea that took United Nations troops to the borders of China. Utopianism, pacifism, and cynical realism more than once have been comingled in the thinking of an individual leader, as with the respected senator from Ohio, the senior Robert Taft, who in the 1940s opposed American participation in NATO and questioned our involvement in the United Nations while simultaneously favoring an international regime based on the rule of law. Secretary of State John Foster Dulles, as chairman of the Commission on International Relations of the National Council of Churches, supported universality of membership for the United Nations, including the admission of Communist China. Yet as secretary of state he was the author of a foreign policy dedicated to rolling back the Soviet sphere of influence in eastern Europe if need be through "massive retaliation," "liberation," and "brinksmanship."

Nor have the politicians or statesmen had any monopoly in the espousal of mutually conflicting if not contradictory political and moral views. Robert Tucker of Johns Hopkins University, a student of Hans Kelsen who was the founder of the pure theory of law, criticized the amoralism of the political realists in the 1950s, but by the 1970s Tucker was proposing a preemptive strike against the oil rich Gulf states in the Arab-Israeli conflict. Hans J. Morgenthau, the leading proponent of negotiations and accommodation with the Russians in the 1950s, became one of Secretary Kissinger's critics in the 1970s for his foreign policy of detente. David Easton, of the faculty of the University of Chicago, announced in the 1950s that all the fundamental answers to the understanding and practice of politics were to be found in the behavioral sciences but later changed his mind and wrote of the need for new insights and approaches in what he christened the postbehavioral era. Arthur Schlesinger, Jr., wrote through the Roosevelt-Truman, Eisenhower, and Kennedy-Johnson years of the need for strong executive leadership; yet the Nixon presidency provoked him to condemn in the most devastating terms the "Imperial Presidency." International lawyers who in the interwar period linked the future of mankind to the growth of a system of universal international law were far more likely in the 1950s, 1960s, and 1970s to approach principles of law as they applied to regional and functional problems such as those of the European Community and the law of the seas. If, as Ralph Waldo Emerson suggested, consistency is the mark of little minds, by this standard most American politicians and political scientists (including myself) would appear to be giants.

Three Perspectives on
the Ethical Problem
in War and Peace

It should be clear from the examples above that statesmen and scholars have been more successful in proclaiming what is right and wrong in international relations and politics than in sustaining their views consistently and coherently over any significant period of time. We seek to do what is right and to follow ethical precepts, but the question that haunts us is "What is Right?" Most of us are all too conscious of the inescapable character of ethical dilemmas in our personal lives. The difficulty of perceiving what is right, however baffling this may be, is surpassed in complexity and uncertainty by the impossibility of foreseeing all the consequences of human actions. The history of men and nations makes it abundantly clear that good and decent men often make choices in good faith and with honest intent that bring on appalling consequences for themselves and the world. Chamberlain at Munich, following the dictates of a responsible Birmingham businessman, sought to strike a bargain with Hitler to preserve the peace of Europe. Historians looking back to his policy, though differing in emphasis, view his approach as a contributory cause of World War II with its unspeakable brutalities and carnage. (It should in fairness be noted that his policy and motives are still being debated by historians.) Churchill by contrast, with a rather vainglorious concept of the British Empire and a quite limited perspective on the rights of dependent peoples, successfully organized and united the Grand Alliance to defend and preserve Western civilization. Franklin D. Roosevelt continues to receive harsh words and disparagement as a leader devoid of all moral and political convictions from such revisionist historians as Gabriel Kolko. Yet not only his wartime leadership but his New Deal economic policies helped avert political and economic catastrophe. (Reinhold Niebuhr in his last years often said that Roosevelt had saved the republic; but Niebuhr also confessed that he had twice voted against FDR because he, in Roosevelt's first years, considered him superficial.) The contrast between Niebuhr who had the courage to change his mind and Kolko who didn't is instructive. Ideologues (who have every right to be heard) are not the best judges of the future. Throughout American history, good men have often initiated policies that produced or hastened disaster. Herbert Hoover, a decent and honorable leader, may not have caused the Great Depression, but his policies did little to prevent a deteriorating situation from growing worse. By contrast men whose intentions were suspect or morally ambiguous have often taken actions that brought about positive results. Lyndon B. Johnson, as a Texan, was not the first choice of blacks or other minorities, but more civil rights legislation was concluded in his years as president than in those of any chief executive before or since.

Faced with the problem of the ambiguity of good and evil, American writers on the ethical dimension of international relations group themselves into at least three distinct categories: the *cynics*, the *utopians*, and the *ideologists*. Ethics, say the cynics, has little if anything to do with war and peace. Most decisions in foreign policy are made either with no reference to ethical principles or are determined by the harsh necessities of international politics where force and fraud prevail. Beginning in the late 1940s, a spate of books and articles by foreign policy practitioners have appeared in the United States, reiterating a common theme. The authors of these studies, deservedly earning public respect and trust, report that for most of the decisions they helped to make, they cannot recall anyone raising the issue of morality. Instead the overwhelming proportion of such choices involved practical questions such as whether to grant or not grant diplomatic recognition to a new or changing government, to issue or not issue a visa, or to undertake or not undertake programs of economic assistance or cultural exchange. The data they were called upon to evaluate involved matters of fact such as whether foreign governments exercised control within given territorial boundaries, whether American citizens traveling abroad could be protected by their government, and whether treaties or agreements acceptable to the participating governments could be successfully negotiated. It may be stretching a point to describe the authors of this approach as cynics, yet the implications of some of their viewpoints have been interpreted thus.

More clearcut expressions of moral cynicism occur in those writings which view international relations almost entirely as a matter of adversary relations. Nation-states are laws unto themselves. They are locked in mortal struggle. Their rivalry can best be described as protracted conflict. Given the incompatibility of their goals and interests, their differences can be resolved only by war, whether it be a hot or cold war. Their relations, contrasting with the shared values of eighteenth- and nineteenth-century monarchs and rulers who constituted a self-conscious aristocratic elite, proceed without benefit of moral consensus. The example most often cited as characteristic of the earlier period is Frederick the Great, who always spoke better French than German. Comparison is frequently made between the relative civility of international relationships among such rulers and the fierce polemics of Soviet and American leaders in the Cold War. Viewing the latter, cynics ask where is the ethical dimension in present-day international relationships.

Utopian writers who study contemporary statecraft agree with the cynics on at least one point. As presently constituted the international system promotes force and violence, not peace and justice. The need, therefore, is to transform the system. However, utopians divide among themselves on at least two basic issues. Some believe in the improvement if not the perfectibility of institutions, provoking the historian Carl Becker to ask *How New Will the Better World Be?* Others believe in the perfectibility of man. Illustrative of the first viewpoint is the utopianism of some who have espoused world government; an example of the latter is the thought underlying certain social-psychological or economic approaches that regard man as good and society as evil. Change society and/or the social circumstances under which men live and their natures will be transformed as a consequence.

Those who espouse utopianism may be separated into soft and hard utopians. The "soft" utopians assert that every political ideol-

33

ogy at root is basically the same. Each serves only a part of mankind, although mankind's needs and interests are everywhere the same. Sooner or later, nation-states will learn this and voluntarily consent to a common regime for mankind. The pathway, as the soft utopians see it, to such a regime is through national choice largely free of the taint of domination or coercion.

"Hard" utopians, on the other hand, insist that one political system is unmistakably superior, that men and nations outside it may from ignorance or false precepts resist. But the righteous and the committed, having been summoned by history, must instruct and if necessary coerce those who are backward and wrongheaded. To this end, the chosen few have a sacred mission, whether they are in the vanguard of the proletariat, the party of liberty, or the more self-righteous of Third World nations. And tragically, history records that, having begun to pursue their mission by preaching and teaching, they may ultimately be tempted toward conflict and coercion, sometimes even toward holy wars, living by fire and the sword because their cause is pure.

Finally, ideologists join with the cynics in affirming that genuine moral purpose in foreign policy is an illusion. They part company with the cynics, however, in insisting that broad moral statements serve a valued purpose. Nations and their leaders act from hard and cynical practical interests, but their success depends on covering their interests with a tissue of ideological and moral justification. Here again the ideologists group themselves in two separate aggregations. For one group, ideologies are no more than a means to an end. However selfish and cynical their goals, national leaders use ideological means to give their acts an ethical justification. They make the worst appear the better cause. For another group of ideologists, including some communist and religious spokesmen, ideology is an end in itself—and it is the sole end and purpose that groups and nations follow in shaping their policies toward other nations. According to this view, China or the Soviet Union act not as traditional nation-states, but as the instruments and purveyors of a single dominant ideology. They are the select vehicles of history, carrying forward a high political and moral creed. Their decisions are the product not of selfish calculations based on national interests but of the ongoing historical process and the advance of the ideology they represent.

Single and Multiple Factor
Analysis in Ethics

There is a more fundamental distinction to be made, however, in characterizing different American approaches to the ethical dimension of war and peace. It is by and large true that most statesmen and thinkers who have concerned themselves with morality and international affairs have fallen within one or the other of two prevailing schools of thought. If we employ terms that have been used in another context by political theorists and theologians, one group may be designated monists and the other pluralists. Monists have found the answer to the question of right and wrong in international relationships by focusing attention on a single moral value; pluralists have chosen to relate one value or set of values to other values in the decision-making process.

In the interwar period, the dominant approach in American universities and colleges was that of international law and organization. Following the repudiation of the League of Nations by the Senate of the United States, a widespread sense of guilt swept over the intellectual community. Scholars took the lead in promoting renewed commitment to American responsibility in world affairs. Practically every chair in international relations was occupied by professors of international law. The mandate of this professoriat, often explicitly stated, was not only the study of the subject but also the advancement of the principle and practice of international law. A remarkable group of scholars, including such men as George Grafton Wilson, Charles C. Hyde, James Berdahl, Quincy Wright, and James Shotwell, accepted the call to become spokesmen for and missionaries of international law.

It is instructive in this connection to reread the publications of the Conferences of Teachers of International Law and Related Subjects sponsored by the Carnegie Endowment for International Peace.

The main thrust of the conferences was plainly the inculcating of widespread scholarly support for international law. A handful of marginal thinkers apparently felt compelled to introduce dissenting opinions to this dominant viewpoint, but they were for the most part voices crying in the wilderness. Noteworthy among them were Nicholas J. Spykman who championed the sociological approach to international law, arguing that law must be studied in relation to wider social and political forces, and Hans J. Morgenthau, whose writings at the time dealt primarily with the limitations of international law. This little group made common cause with such American scholars as John Bassett Moore and Edwin Borchard, such British writers as George W. Keeton and Georg Schwarzenburger of London University, and such European jurists as Charles de Visscher. It is difficult to escape the conclusion, however, that most influential international lawyers in the 1930s were monists in their approach to international values.

Among statesmen, a similar concentration on single values was apparent. The pre-presidential writings of Woodrow Wilson, to which historians such as Arthur Link and Arthur Walworth have called attention, demonstrate that the great reformist president was acutely aware of the vagaries of American politics. He saw the inevitable struggle between the Congress and the president in the shaping of public policy. Conspicuous by its absence in his great work, *Congressional Government*, was any significant discussion of foreign policy; yet this was the sphere in which Wilson as president can most convincingly be judged a monist. Not only did he defend the League of Nations as a panacea in the resolution of world problems (John Maynard Keynes, Walter Lippmann, Sir Harold Nicolson, and others in writings on the Paris Peace Conference have pointed up Wilson's supreme indifference to the complexities of settling the hard questions of territorial boundaries in Europe), but he saw the doctrine of national self-determination as the single important value for resolving conflicts among nations. He was seemingly oblivious to the high price of nationalism inherent in the economic consequences of the breakup of the Austro-Hungarian Empire in the heart of Europe. Another Wilsonian, Cordell Hull, the congressman from

Tennessee, who would become secretary of state under Franklin D. Roosevelt, substituted freedom of international trade as the single value for resolving conflicts among nations. Trade rather than nationalism was to bring international strife to an end.

In opposition to the monist approach, other thinkers and political leaders have adopted a pluralist perspective on values. In this they have drawn on the ancient tradition of moral reasoning. Hannah Arendt, one of the few American political philosophers in the mid-twentieth century whose writings promise to have enduring value, summoned political scientists to reexamine the Platonic dialogues. In her lectures and in a series of little-known articles, including one of classic proportions in *Social Research*,[1] Arendt pointed out that Socrates approached the great issues of values through conversations between individuals of divergent political views. To such individuals, Socrates posed timeless questions regarding justice, virtue, and the good state. Their conversations characteristically took the form of what may seem little more than meandering reflections on the many facets of the question of right and wrong. Their reflections and debates left most of the basic issues unresolved. But having uncovered the contradictions and complexities of moral reasoning about the great issues of the nature of man and the state and pointing out to the participants that they had come full circle, Socrates said, "Let us start over again and think about our problems in a new light." Hannah Arendt insisted that out of this seemingly wandering and inconclusive discourse, new levels of understanding emerged. The moral problem as Socrates viewed it was not to be solved once and for all; it required continuous reexamination.

In another realm of political discourse, Paul Freund, renowned Carl M. Loeb University Professor of Constitutional Law at Harvard, has been an exemplar of the pluralist approach. Values in law and politics, Freund has stated, cluster and compete with one another. The choice of right or wrong is seldom one involving action based upon a single good. Choice in law and politics commonly involves discriminate judgment between competing goods. Rights compete with rights, and justice for one man or group can mean injustice for another; moral reasoning, therefore, involves an unending process of

37

balancing competing rights and interests. In politics and law, men are required to live without benefit of absolute truth. For every truth there is a balancing truth; only demagogues or fanatics are freed of such constraints. Reporters covering courtroom trials affirm the rights of a free press and the public's right to know, but American constitutional law also provides for a fair trial for defendants. The peculiarities of the American system of trial by a jury presumed to be impartial throughout the trial, unswayed by public passions, set limits to premature public disclosure. Those limits conflict with freedom of the press.

The problem of competing values runs the gamut of war and peace issues. There is widespread popular appeal in the Wilsonian doctrine of "open covenants openly arrived at." Monists have always addressed themselves to the evils of secret diplomacy, and congressmen have railed against the lack of full and open disclosure regarding negotiations by the executive branch of government with leaders of other states. (Diplomatic columnists have speculated that Secretary of State Kissinger spent substantial time out of the country partly to escape continuous questioning and scrutiny by the numerous committees of Congress on delicate and sensitive negotiations with foreign powers.) Walter Lippmann frequently reminded his readers that individuals, not assemblies, are alone capable of diplomatic negotiations. The limited truth of the Wilsonian formula of "open covenants" is evident in its subsequent modification to read "open covenants secretly negotiated."

Monism in Contemporary Ethical Thought

The clash between the monist and pluralist outlooks may take on more specific and concrete meaning if we examine a few of the popularly held philosophies of war and peace, considering the ways in which they have been tested and applied to important issues.

1. THREE PHILOSOPHIES OF WAR AND PEACE: EMPHASIZING THE SINGLE FACTOR *Pacifism* stands out among the leading war and

peace theories as perhaps the most attractive to liberal and humane people. It selects from the range of possible objectives nations may pursue in foreign policy one fundamental aim—the quest for peace. Distinction is sometimes made between absolute and pragmatic pacifists, the latter being more inclined to take part in social and humanitarian endeavors in devastated areas or inside oppressed societies. The merit of pacifism lies in its providing a noble example of human behavior for others to emulate. Its weakness lies, in the words of Reinhold Niebuhr, in trying to make "a success story of the Cross." Norman Thomas, the Socialist party candidate for president in successive presidential elections, may be the best-known American political leader to embrace pacifism, though various local and regional leaders have been outspoken advocates of the doctrine, and the American Friends Service Committee and the Fellowship for Reconciliation have made considerable headway in institutionalizing it. Scholars like Kenneth Boulding, Clark Kerr, and Gilbert White and publicists like the indestructible A. J. Muste have gained the respect of pacifists and nonpacifists alike. No one in the United States has achieved the towering political heights of Gandhi in India, and it is fair to ask whether this great leader's political strategy could have succeeded if Germany or the Soviet Union had been the ruling colonial power rather than Britain. In international politics, the Bandung Conference states of India, Indonesia, Egypt, and Yugoslavia in the 1950s, with their common commitment to "neutralism," have come closer to pacifism than any recent American foreign policy. Since the days of the Bandung Conference, however, the signatory states have drifted farther from pacifism. Switzerland's neutrality is made possible by a combination of citizen military preparedness and a favorable geographical environment.

Militarism occupies a place at the opposite end of the spectrum. It is not difficult to show that it too has concentrated on a single factor. For a country that in modern times has had an aversion to standing armies, the United States in the mid-twentieth century has done an abrupt about-face. Military expenditures, averaging considerably above one hundred billion dollars, are second only to those of the Department of Health, Education, and Welfare. The trend toward militarism had gone so far by the 1950s that President Dwight D. Eisenhower saw fit in his farewell address to warn against the mounting power of the military-industrial complex. Administration spokesmen who went before congressional committees found that economic assistance programs were more likely to be accepted when they were linked with military assistance. Pentagon officials have on many occasions opposed concessions that diplomats were contemplating because in the armed forces lexicon political advantages took distinctly second place to military superiority. Retired Admiral and Chief of Naval Operations Elmo Zumwalt fought a campaign for the Senate on the principal issue of a decline in military preparedness.

Peace through economic development and human rights is a third and for many a more convincing expression of single factor analysis. It is rooted in the belief that war comes about primarily as a result of economic disparities among peoples or gross violations of human rights. While the coupling of the two forms of monism in peace theories may appear arbitrary and even contradictory, it has often been true in the United States that the same individuals and organizations have been supporters of the two approaches. Thus Father Theodore Hesburgh, president of the University of Notre Dame, has written and spoken with forceful eloquence on the need for increased technical assistance to the developing countries while at the same time spearheading the drive for human rights around the world. The Overseas Development Council in Washington has chosen as twin focal points for its efforts economic development and human rights. Not only are these goals congenial to the liberal spirit of many Americans, but they happen to coincide with the principal goals of the republic. And much as Woodrow Wilson was persuaded that the goals of America were the goals of all mankind, present-day champions trumpet not peace or international understanding as a goal but the establishment of human rights. In the words of Senator Daniel Patrick Moynihan of New York: "The case for making human rights concerns fundamental to our foreign policy is twofold. First, these are the issues we care most about, or ought to care most about. . . . But second, there is a profound strategic point. To press human rights is to press the natural advantage of the United States. For we, and a few like us, maintain free societies, while most of the nations of the world do not." Senator Moynihan goes on to support his cause by citing a Freedom House survey quantified to his delight and showing that there are forty–one free nations in the world, of which two are in South America, two in Africa, two in Asia. (On the numbers, he comments parenthetically, "The virtue of human rights as an issue is that it is . . . quantifiable: morality can mean anything and hence usually means nothing.") And, the Senator concluded, "If we are to adopt the human rights standard, it must be a single-standard. No distinction between aid that helps the poor as against other kinds. None of these distinctions bear scrutiny." [2] In other words, American foreign policy ought to rest on a single factor.

American Foreign Policy
Problems and Monism

1. PEACE IN VIETNAM   "Peace in Vietnam" was the battle cry of the critics of American policy in Vietnam, especially among those who were in the vanguard of the youth movement. A full assessment of what some have come to call the Vietnam debacle remains the task of future historians. The main question, regarding the initiation of the defense of Vietnam, proliferates into related questions such as the connection between that country and the opening up of relations with China. There is bitter irony in the fact that the public debate over our Vietnamese policy was between two contending absolutist viewpoints—one grounded in the belief that peace ought to be our sole objective in Vietnam and the other that aggression anywhere in the world must be halted. The necessity of resistance to aggression was the lesson taught us by the belated response of the Allies to Hitler's imperialism. For a whole generation of policy-makers no other principle of foreign policy was needed. This was the litmus paper to be applied in judging policy recommendations on any problem that arose involving a threat to peace in any area of the world, whatever the political concerns.

Inevitably, a Thermidorean reaction set in. If resisting aggression everywhere in the world was the thesis, peace at any price was the antithesis. Once the commitment to intervene in Vietnam had been made, a host of questions and interrelated issues bore in on the policy-makers—beginning with an assessment of the interests, objectives, and capacities of the major participants in the struggle and branching out into strategic issues involving Chinese and Soviet interests and capacities in the region. One need not construct an overall defense of the Kennedy-Johnson or the Nixon-Ford foreign policy to say that any administration and any group of public officials pursuing the national interest would have been obliged to take many factors into account, including the much criticized slogan "peace with honor." It was easier to decide we should never have intervened than to know how to disengage once we became involved. The Vietnam issue was less a question of a handful of misguided leaders than the clarification of the requirements of national security.

To all this, the leaders of the peace movement remained largely indifferent. It was a sign of the nature and character of the movement that it disintegrated, once peace was achieved, although the need for peace in Berlin, the Middle East, and South Africa has continued. Ending the bloodshed in Vietnam—a worthy moral and political purpose—was an end in itself. It brought about a public response powerful enough to terminate the political life and ambitions of President Johnson. But based on a single consideration, peace in that Southeast Asian country was not sufficient to provide the basis for an ongoing foreign policy.

2. MILITARISM IN KOREA The Korean War throws light on the hazards of another kind of single factor analysis. After World War II the United States had dismantled its military establishment to its lowest point since the interwar period. Our commitments to South Korea and those of other members of the United Nations required that the invasion from the north be turned back. What began as a limited military buildup soon led to actions requiring that the defense budget be raised to a level approaching thirty billion dollars. The initial commitment to contain expansion from the north had as its corollary the assurance that China would not intervene and that

the United States not be drawn into a land war on the mainland of China. The enemy was North Korea and every precaution was to be taken that China not be provoked to enter the conflict.

Once the struggle was joined, however, and battlefield considerations and requirements became dominant, the military and the brilliant field commander, General Douglas MacArthur, assumed full authority. Korea was far away, and the exigencies of battle were such that MacArthur was granted, or interpreted his orders as giving him, *carte blanche*. A war begun in part as a struggle to restore political equilibrium in the regime became almost exclusively a military struggle. Only when it was too late and China entered the war was the power of the Commander in Chief, President Truman, restored. Whatever the elements in the thinking of civilian and military authorities that brought the situation about, a military, not a political, approach was maintained until the removal of MacArthur. Militarism had prevailed to that point as the principal basis of foreign policy.

3. TECHNICAL ASSISTANCE AND THE MAJORITY POOR If a growing militarism has been one characteristic of American foreign policy since World War II, another has been the attempt by Americans to use their vast material resources to help less fortunate peoples cope with their most vexing problems. Some observers have characterized technical assistance programs as a secularization of the missionary movement. Others point to enlightened self-interest as a primary motivation. Over a thirty-year period the technical assistance effort has continued with some programs being more successful than others. Beginning in the mid-1970s, a strenuous effort has been made to channel a far higher proportion of aid to the majority poor in the developing countries. In bilateral programs and in multilateral efforts such as those of the World Bank, emphasis has shifted from country programs or attempts to build more viable structures and institutions for economic and educational growth toward new designs for helping the poor. Recipient countries have been put on notice that any assistance given them must be directed to the needs of the more numerous poor rather than drained off by the wealthy few at the top.

What began, however, as a worthwhile reorientation of foreign aid has brought growing criticism on several fronts. Leaders of some of the developing countries point the finger at American spokesmen whom they find guilty of moral hypocrisy. Americans have failed to solve the problem of the poor at home (according to an estimate in the mid-1970s, the lowest 10 percent have 1.5 percent of the wealth while the top 10 percent have 26 percent). Yet when foreign governments such as India under Madame Gandhi, Chile under Salvador Allende, Jamaica, Tanzania, and Cuba set out on a drastic new course intended to help the poor, they are the first countries we repudiate and ignore. Friends in the developing countries are also frank to say that the United States has had two hundred years in which to solve its problems, whereas they have been struggling with theirs for no more than ten to twenty-five years. Their most serious criticism, though, is that help to the poor requires policies, programs, and the necessary infrastructure; and these will not emerge full-blown as from the mind of Zeus. For a decade or two Americans have helped the developing countries build new institutions, for example, in higher education; and now that they are beginning to show signs of meeting the nation's most urgent needs, we announce that we have no interest in higher education but only in helping the majority poor in as yet undefined programs of basic education.

4. HUMAN RIGHTS AND DETENTE The most controversial case of choosing to deal with one moral question in isolation from all the rest concerns the plight of the Jews in Russia. A growing awareness of the persecution by the Soviet government of this minority group has coincided with the foreign policy of detente initiated for the United States by President Nixon and Secretary Kissinger. Few responsible people debate the need for relaxation of tensions in Soviet-American relations, though specific questions have understandably arisen as to whether American negotiators have conceded too much. The Jackson-Vanik amendment, however, was designed to link the granting of favorable trade arrangements with relaxation of emigration rights of Soviet Jews. Available diplomatic reports indicate that Secretary Kissinger had come to a tacit understanding with the Kremlin concerning the emigration of such people. The

Jackson-Vanik amendment made impossible the implementation of this confidential agreement. In part the debate has centered on a question of facts with Senator Jackson arguing that public pressure on the Soviets will increase the number of Jews given permission to leave while Secretary Kissinger, John Kenneth Galbraith, and others have maintained that influential private contacts are more helpful and that emigration has fallen off sharply since the Jackson-Vanik amendment. The heart of the debate, however, has to do with priorities in foreign policy and whether the human rights of one minority group should determine the fate of a major foreign policy initiative such as detente. Holding to the single factor of human rights puts all other issues, including detente, into a secondary position.

Moral Reasoning as an Alternative Approach

The somewhat bleak picture that emerges from a review of philosophies and policies that base ethical thinking on a single moral principle or goal is, fortunately, only half the story. Particularly since World War II, a significant group of thinkers has appeared on the American scene; and their writings fall broadly within the tradition of moral reasoning. Each has attracted his share of followers and critics. All have tended in their work, whatever their limitations, to direct attention to the multiple factors that affect moral reasoning. At the same time, they have attempted to rank such factors in order, not being content with the characteristically generalized statement Cyrus Vance made in his first televised press conference as secretary of state—that "morality is an aspect of foreign policy." In this, Secretary Vance, like most of his predecessors, was less than illuminating in describing his personal ordering of values.

1. REINHOLD NIEBUHR   The first of these thinkers is the theologian, Reinhold Niebuhr. In a vast outpouring of thought and writing that began in 1929 with *Leaves from the Notebook of a Tamed Cynic,* Niebuhr has brooded about and sought to clarify the relation between ethics or religion and society.[3]

George F. Kennan has called Niebuhr "the father of us all." If

45

Niebuhr is the father of this intellectual tradition that Kennan and others have followed, his children have chosen to interpret him in many diverse ways. Religious people who take pride in Niebuhr's commitment to what he called "Christian realism" may prefer to forget his words, "Religion is a good thing for honest people but a bad thing for dishonest people . . . and the church has not been impressive because many of its leaders rationalize."[4]

Secular leaders were attracted to Niebuhr by the score, perhaps because of what he called his "dialogue with doubt." A group at Harvard called itself "atheists for Niebuhr." This and similar groups must have been embarassed by words he quoted, "No matter how far back I go . . . I cannot get back to an atheistic mentality. As little can I reach a day when I was conscious of myself but not of God as I can reach a day when I was conscious of myself but not of other human beings."[5]

This unique combination of a critical and a religious perspective made Niebuhr both the forerunner of other critical thinkers and an irreplaceable figure on the American intellectual scene. At the 1974 meeting of the American Political Science Association attended by five hundred scholars, Arthur Schlesinger, Jr., summed up the views of a panel discussing Niebuhr's contribution, saying: "No one has taken his place or the role he performed from the 1930's to the 1960's."

Niebuhr sought to link his study of history and politics with a theory of human nature. His criticism of contemporary political science centered on its insistence that political theory was rooted in political institutions and statistically verifiable behavior rather than in any historic view of the human condition, for he felt that any understanding of political phenomena is inseparable from the search for the intrinsic qualities of man. His celebrated Gifford Lectures began: "Man has always been his most vexing problem. How shall he think of himself?" Then Niebuhr went on in a mode of dialectical thought that was to characterize all his writings on the ethical dimensions of politics, saying that any affirmation about man involves conflicts and contradictions. If the observer stresses man's unique and rational qualities, then man's greed, lust for power, and brute

46

nature betray him. If the writer holds that men everywhere are the product of nature and unable to rise above circumstances, this tells us nothing of the man who dreams of God and of making himself God, nor of the man whose sympathy knows no bounds. If the student of history declares that man is essentially good and attributes all evil to concrete historical and social causes, he merely begs the question, for these causes are revealed, on scrutiny, to be the consequences of the evil inherent in man. If he concludes that man is bereft of all virtue, his very capacity for reaching such a judgment refutes his conclusion. All these perplexing conflicts in human self-knowledge point up the difficulty of doing justice simultaneously to the uniqueness of man and to his affinities with nature. The heart of Niebuhr's criticism is that modern views of man which stress exclusively either his dignity or his misery are fatuous and irrelevant, as they fail to consider the good and evil, the dualism in man's nature.

The deeper paradox arises from the fact that man is suspended perilously between freedom and finiteness, spirit and nature, the human and the divine. His ambiguous and contradictory position at the juncture of freedom and finiteness produces in him a condition of anxiety that is fundamental to understanding political behavior. Man is anxious about the imperialism of others, yet secretly fearful of his own vulnerability and limitations. Because of the finiteness of his reason, he can never wholly judge his own possibilities. So he endlessly seeks security in the pretense that he has overcome his finiteness, his human limitations. Only through extending his power and influence is he safeguarded against the domination of others.

The most important observable expression of human anxiety politically is seen in the will to power. With animals man shares natural appetites and desires, along with an impulse for survival. Yet being both human and divine, deriving his powers from nature and spirit, his requirements are qualitatively heightened; they are raised irretrievably to the level of spirit where they become limitless and insatiable. To overcome social anxiety, man seeks power and control over his fellows, endeavoring to subdue them lest they come to dominate him. The struggle for political power is merely an example of the rivalry that goes on at every level of human life. It manifests

47

itself in relations between husbands and wives; parents and children; spouses and in-laws; ethnic groups; children and remarried parents; cities, states, and the nation; and the executive and legislative branches of government.

In collective behavior the force of egoistic passion is so strong that the only harmonies possible are those which manage to neutralize a rival force through balances of power, through mutual defenses against the inordinate expression of power, and through techniques for harnessing its energy toward social ends. Social unity is built on the virtuous as well as the selfish side of man's nature; the twin elements of collective strength for a nation become self-sacrificial loyalty and the frustrated aggression of the masses. From this it follows that politics is the more contentious and ruthless because of the unselfish loyalty and commitments of group members, loyalties that become laws unto themselves, unrestrained by their obedient and worshipful members. Niebuhr's conclusion is that within international society, even a nation composed of men of the greatest good will is less than loving toward other nations. He observes: "Society ... merely cumulates the egoism of individuals and transmutes their individual altruism into collective egoism so that the egoism of the group has a double force. For this reason no group acts from purely unselfish or even mutual interest, and politics is therefore bound to be a contest of power."[6] (The equivalent of this statement appears in almost every book by Niebuhr.)

Translating this to the level of world politics, nations pursue the quest for power, influence, and prestige, heightened by the intensity of collective loyalties that are compounded by present-day alienations and frustrations. All nations claim they seek security and follow their national interest; Niebuhr is willing to concede that nations on the whole are not particularly generous; a wise self-interest is usually the limit of their moral attainment. The demands of self-interest and national self-protection lead to acts that appear to override all accepted moral impulses. The decision in the early 1950s to build the hydrogen bomb gave offense to many sensitive people. But Niebuhr agreed that no nation would deny itself the means of defense if the alternative to not arming itself was the risk of subjugation. Yet even as he took this stand, Niebuhr was terrified and appalled by the prospect of nuclear proliferation.

Niebuhr was persuaded that men and states cannot follow their self-interest without claiming to do so in obedience to some general scheme of values. This belief led him to ask whether a consistent and unquestioning emphasis upon the national interest is not as self-defeating in a nation as it is in a person's life. Stated differently, does not a nation exclusively concerned with its own interests define those interests so narrowly that the very interests and securities, which depend on common devotion to principles of justice and established mutualities in the community of nations, are sacrificed? In American foreign policy, we claim more for the benevolence of our policies than they deserve, heightening thereby the resentments of people already envious of our wealth and power. National interest, therefore, is imperiled both by moral cynicism and by moral pretension, hypocrisy, and ideological justification. In his earlier writings, Niebuhr strongly denounced moral cynicism, but later he became more concerned with hypocrisy and ideological justification, concluding that cynicism and pretension were two parts of a single problem. That problem involves our continuing ambivalence toward the moral issue and its principal dimensions, as we claim first that nations have no obligations beyond their interest and then that they are engaged in a high moral crusade without regard for selfish interests.

Edmund Burke provided Niebuhr with a concept that became central to the last stages of the great theologian's thinking. Theorists, and more particularly "scientists" of society, have often given themselves over to the belief that the historical realm is analogous to the realm of nature and that the adoption of proper scientific or theoretical techniques will assure man mastery over his historical fate. Most scientific studies have thus been largely irrelevant to the practice of statecraft, where the watchword must be "sufficient unto the day is the evil thereof." For Burke, the problem of relating theory and practice in politics is bound up with the concept of prudence. Prudence, not justice, is first in the rank of political virtues; it is the director and regulator. Metaphysics cannot live without definition, but prudence is cautious in its definitions, for it has learned to live with ever-changing reality. As Niebuhr moved toward an increasingly more pragmatic view of world politics, he sensed the limits of rational as well as traditional normative thinking. In the largely irrational realm of politics, the struggle is usually so intense that the only possible peace becomes an armistice and the only order a provisional balance among forces. Even the proximate moral norms of politics are seldom realized in practice; statesmen must settle for uncertain compromises. It is as necessary to moderate the moral pretensions of every contestant in the power struggle as it is to make moral distinctions regarding the national interest. In the 1920s Niebuhr was a social reformer and optimist; in the Marxist 1930s he was a radical; but in his later years he became a Christian realist. When critics warned that he was in danger of being little more than a pragmatist, he replied that his pragmatism was limited and instrumental, even while acknowledging that through it he risked standing "on the abyss of cynicism." What saved him from this position, he hoped, was his openness to criticism by friend, foe, and God. It was also his ability through religion and, in the American constitutional system, through the higher law—to stand outside the world of events "in order to get a fulcrum on it." He paraphrased St. Paul in *Irony of American History:* "Nothing worth doing is completed in our lifetime; therefore we must be saved by hope. . . . Nothing we do, however virtuous, can be accomplished alone; therefore we are saved by love. No virtuous act is quite as virtuous from the standpoint of our friend or foe as from our standpoint. Therefore, we must be saved by the final form of love which is forgiveness."[7]

2. HANS J. MORGENTHAU Another writer who attributes much of the development of his thinking to Niebuhr is Hans J. Morgenthau. His classic text, *Politics Among Nations,* has educated several generations of students and practitioners in the realities of world politics. That he wrote with such candor about the harsher aspects of poli-

tics cloaked an underlying compassion. At the end of a conference of
theorists in Washington Walter Lippmann said to Morgenthau: "You
are not the hard-headed realist you are painted but the most moral
man I know." Morgenthau's writings, like Niebuhr's, are voluminous;
they include contributions both in political theory and foreign policy:
*Scientific Man vs. Power Politics; In Defense of the National Interest;
Principles and Problems of International Politics; The Purpose of
American Politics; Dilemmas of Politics; A New Foreign Policy for the
United States;* and *Politics in the 20th Century.*

Morgenthau, more than any American scholar, sought to turn
American thinking on war and peace from its preoccupation with
laws and structures to its core in international politics. For him as for
Niebuhr, politics at bedrock is a struggle for power. In the present
world system, power and interests are linked with the security of
the nation-state, but nowhere is it preordained that nation-states
remain as the permanent political units of international society. The
paradox of the present era is that nation-states have become obsolete
in providing for the most urgent needs of man, but no other unit has
emerged effectively to replace them. The nation-state will not disappear, whatever its weaknesses, until something better is available to
take its place.

In this vein of thought, Morgenthau has remained skeptical of
every other device or instrumentality proposed for doing away with
the struggle for power. *Power politics,* when this man set forth on
his career in the United States, were dirty and forbidden words.
Politics was something world government or public administration
were designed to eradicate. Politics epitomized all that was evil and
had to be uprooted if men were to live in a civilized world. To these
judgments Morgenthau responded in the most uncompromising
terms, saying: "Whatever the ultimate aims of international politics,
power is always the immediate aim. Statesmen and people may ultimately seek freedom, security, prosperity or power itself. They may
define their goals in terms of a religious, philosophic, economic or
social ideal.... But whenever they strive to realize their goal by
means of international politics, they do so by striving for power."[8]

51

To those who took issue with him, maintaining that power politics had not always existed and need not exist in the future, he answered:

> The struggle for power is universal in time and place and is an undeniable fact of experience. . . . Even though anthropologists have shown that certain primitive people seem to be free from the desire for power, nobody has yet shown how their state of mind and the conditions under which they live can be recreated on a worldwide scale. . . . It would be useless and even self-destructive to free one or the other of the peoples of the earth from the desire for power while leaving it extant in others. If the desire for power cannot be abolished everywhere in the world, those who might be cured would simply fall victim to the power of others.[9]

Having rejected the optimistic views of those who predicted the end of power politics, Morgenthau devoted much of his writings to a discussion of the limitations of national power. He looked to international law, international organization, world community, international cooperation, and national purpose for effecting such limitations. He has had considerable to say about moral consensus within and among nations, and where it has been lacking he has expressed strong doubts about world government or political accommodation.

Furthermore, few writers have had as much to say about the clash of values and the interplay between values and interests. Where moral consensus is lacking among states, the best to be hoped for is a provisional accommodation of their interests and, failing this, a redefinition of their interests. Treaties and agreements, Morgenthau says, must register an existing situation of facts; they cannot be imposed when the respective national interests of allies or foes are in conflict with one another. Soviet-American relations pointedly illustrate the conspicuous absence of such consensus, a fact that at least in part is the cause of Morgenthau's skepticism about detente.

More than Niebuhr, Morgenthau is inclined to say that politics most often involves a choice of lesser evils. There are fateful choices that involve not so much the balancing of rights against rights as judgments about which course of action is least likely to bring harmful results. Morgenthau's essentially tragic view of the course of action open to statesmen is based on his belief that two factors have brought about the deterioration of moral limitations on power: the substitution of democratic for aristocratic responsibility in foreign affairs and of nationalistic standards of action for universal ones. On the former, he writes: "Moral rules have their seat in the conscience of individual men.... Where responsibility for government is widely distributed among a great number of individuals with different conceptions as to what is morally required in international affairs, or with no conception at all, international morality as an effective system of restraints upon international policy becomes impossible."[10] In support of his views, he cites Roscoe Pound, who wrote: "It might be maintained plausibly, that a moral ... order among states, was nearer attainment in the middle of the eighteenth century than it is today."[11] On the latter change—that is, the substitution of nationalistic for universalistic norms—Morgenthau, having tested the manner in which the universal ethical command, "Thou shalt not kill" is transformed into the national ethic, "Thou shalt kill under certain conditions the enemies of thy country," concludes: "Carrying their idols before them, the nationalistic masses of our time meet in the international arena, each group convinced that it executes the mandate of history, that it does for humanity what it seems to do for itself, and that it fulfills a sacred mission ordained by providence, however defined. Little do they know that they meet under an empty sky from which the Gods have departed."[12]

It is the tragic element in life and politics which, more than any other, preoccupies Morgenthau: men seek power as the means to worthy ends, but mankind and its ends are corrupted by the pursuit of power; ideological foreign policy is a contradiction to successful diplomacy, but foreign policy not rooted in national purpose is aimless; and the national state is obsolete, but no effective world community has yet come into being. Life is lived at the point of such apparent contradictions and antinomies, and to obscure this is sham and sophistry.

3. WALTER LIPPMANN Walter Lippmann began his intellectual journey in seeking to understand the ethical dimension when he

wrote in the first issue of the *New Republic:* "Every sane person
knows it is a greater thing to build a city than to bombard it, to
plough a field than to trample it, to serve mankind than to conquer
it." With Woodrow Wilson, he was persuaded that those who were
prepared to use political reason and moral judgment would see the
futility of war. He began as a socialist and a foe of the European
balance of power. As secretary of the inquiry engaged in preparing
for the peace settlement after World War I, he collaborated in the
formulation of the Fourteen Points.

By February 17, 1917, Lippmann and his colleagues at *New Republic* sought to warn President Wilson that legalism and moralism
were not enough and that an overall political strategy for war and
peace had become essential. He acknowledged that both the block-
ade by the British and submarine warfare by the Germans were
terrible weapons, just as war was terrible. In choosing between them,
however, the United States would not be choosing between illegality
and legality, or even between cruelty and mercy. What mattered was
that because the United States in its own interest could not permit a
German triumph, we accepted the closure of the seas to Germany
and the opening of them to the Allies. Lippmann wrote: "We are an
inveterately legalistic people and have veiled our real intentions
behind a mass of technicalities. . . . We have wanted to assist the
Allies and hamper Germany, but we have wanted also to keep out of
war. Our government therefore has been driven to stretch technicalities to the breaking point. We have clothed the most unneutral purposes in the language of neutrality."[13]

After the war, Lippmann continued his attack on moralistic pro-
nouncements. We were told, he observed, that the United States
would work for justice and peace. Such words are hollow vessels
into which almost anybody can pour anything he chooses. Moral
and political choices involved deciding what was vital in Europe to
a stable peace and our interests. We needed policies that offered
Europe something concrete. Instead, he continued:

> When it came to the test Wilson was to treat American policies
> like so many other ideals, something distant and of no material
> consequence. Calling ourselves disinterested, we behaved as if

we were uninterested, and furnished the world with the extraordinary spectacle of a nation willing to send two million
soldiers overseas, yet unwilling to project its mind and conscience overseas.... When Mr. Wilson began, Europe believed
that the Wilson program was an American program, a thing as
vital to us as Alsace-Lorraine was to France. But in the course of
time the European statemen discovered that Mr. Wilson's program was really nothing more than his gratuitious advice in a
situation he did not thoroughly understand.[14]

The tragedy was that history was to repeat itself. We marched
into Germany in World War II, and once again winning the war
became an end in itself. Just as we had had no policy for the peace
after World War I, this time we had only the vague goal of ending
alliances and the balance of power, things that we categorically la-
beled as the causes of all previous wars. The Russians and the British
had political and territorial goals clearly in mind, though Stalin said
that he, by comparison with Hitler, knew when to stop. We failed to
remember that an international organization, the major goal we
worked for and advanced, cannot write the peace or establish a
territorial status quo which it must defend. It is rather the nations,
partners in war and peace, who must bring this about.

Lippmann's main proposition on the ethics of war and peace was
his belief that ideals and goals can never be approached apart from
political and territorial questions. For in ethics there is always a
political dimension. To forget this is to place ethics on the remote
and ceremonial pedestal of utopian thought.

4. GEORGE F. KENNAN George Kennan's contribution has been to
extend Lippmann's thesis—elaborating, sharpening, and refining it.
The areas of fundamental agreement between these men make
Lippmann's criticism of his formulation of the containment doctrine
in the Cold War even more poignant for Kennan. In *American Diplomacy*, Kennan wrote: "I see the most serious fault ... to lie in
something that I might call the legalistic-moralistic approach to international problems. This approach runs like a red skein through
our foreign policy of the last fifty years." What was this approach? In
Kennan's criticism it was the belief "that it should be possible to

suppress the chaotic and dangerous aspirations of governments in
the international field by . . . legal rules and restraints."

> Instead of taking the awkward conflicts of national interest and
> dealing with them on their merits with a view to finding the
> solutions least unsettling to the stability of international life, it
> would be better to find some formal criteria of a juridical nature
> by which the permissible behavior of states could be defined.
> Behind all this, of course, lies the American assumption that
> the things for which other peoples in this world are likely to
> contend are for the most part neither creditable nor important
> and might justly be expected to take second place behind the
> desirability of an orderly world, untroubled by international
> violence.[15]

What were the reasons for the all-pervasive character of the
legalistic-moralistic approach? In seeking an explanation, Kennan
mentions the dominant role of the legal profession in American
statecraft, as well as a stubborn insistence that all states are like our
own, content with their international borders and status. Legalism
by itself would be a serious impediment to America's understanding of the world. Its association with moralism compounds the difficulty. For moralism involves the carrying over into the affairs of
state the concepts of right and wrong, the assumption, in Kennan's
much-debated phrase, that state behavior is not a fit subject for moral
judgment.

What Kennan would accept as a final interpretation of this phrase
is difficult to know, despite several attempts to clarify it. What he
opposes is clear: the tendency of those who claim that there is a law
on some contemporary problem and are indignant against the lawbreaker and feel a moral superiority over him; the spilling over of
their indignation into the conduct of a military struggle; their impa-
tience until they reduce the lawbreaker to complete submissiveness
and achieve what became the Allies' objective in World War II—
unconditional surrender. Ironically, this approach, rooted in a desire
to do away with war and violence, intensifies violence and makes it
more destructive of political stability than did the older motives of
national interest. A war that is fought in the name of high moral
principle seldom ends before total domination is realized. Kennan is

a moral absolutist on only one count—his denunciation of atomic weapons and war which, he has said, go beyond anything that the Christian ethic can properly accept.

What would Kennan put in the place of the dangerous and damaging approach of wars fought to end wars or for some other moral principle? Despite his skepticism about international law, he would not wish to see it lose respect as "a gentle civilizer of events." What he urges instead is:

> A new attitude among us toward many things outside our borders that are irritating and unpleasant today—an attitude more like that of the doctor toward the physical phenomena in the human body that are neither pleasing nor fortunate—an attitude of detachment and soberness and readiness to reserve judgment . . . the modesty to admit that our own national interest is all that we are really capable of knowing and understanding—and the courage to recognize that if our own purposes and undertakings here at home are decent ones, unsullied by arrogance or hostility toward other people or delusions of superiority, then the pursuit of our national interest can never fail to be conducive to a better world.[16]

CONCLUSION   It should be obvious that the four thinkers considered above are exemplars of pluralism in moral reasoning. Whatever the deficiencies of their thought, they can hardly be judged for paying heed only to a single factor such as peace or military defense. Each in turn has spoken out against exclusive concern for economic development or human rights. All contend that we must first "know ourselves" before we can "know others." On the subject of Korea, they recognized the need, as pacifists did not, for turning back North Korea's invasion and for maintaining a more stable equilibrium of forces in the region. But their criticism was loud and unqualified regarding pursuit of the enemy that was heedless to the threat of drawing China into the struggle and changing the character of a limited war. On the Vietnam War they each questioned from the beginning whether our national interest was involved and whether we grasped the true nature of the conflict, particularly its historical and political roots. On technical assistance and the majority poor,

they doubted, as would Lippmann and Niebuhr had they lived, the
rather utopian view that America by itself could change the economic and demographic map of the world. On detente, it is likely
that all four would favor such a policy, in principle though not
without questioning whether President Nixon and Secretary of State
Kissinger had not oversold it. Three of the four almost certainly
would join the critics of detente in maintaining that concern for
human rights in Russia should be weighed in the balance—but in
the context of the more fundamental need for reduction of tensions
between the United States and the Soviet Union.

However, a score sheet on issues and policies about which the
four thinkers were more prescient than policy-makers or the general
public is not the purpose of this discussion. The real issue to be
pondered is whether their general approach of moral reasoning is
more soundly based and central to the ethical dimension than are the
monistic approaches that have tended to prevail in American thinking. It is their first and their principal merit that they offer us an
alternative perspective—one which has not been tested and found
wanting in American foreign policy so much as ignored and passed
over, one which represents a more hopeful way of thinking about
war and peace and morality than does any prevailing viewpoint.

III

Functionalism and World Order

There may be a certain arbitrariness in selecting for discussion a single approach and theory of international relations. My justification is that functionalism has emerged as one significant way of viewing the needs of an interdependent world. It has also received less attention than approaches that stress national security and its relationship to armaments. With this in mind I have devoted an entire section of this book to functionalism, especially as it illuminates higher education, agriculture, and the role of foundations in the developing world. I have attempted to review the relevance of functionalism measured against realities in these three areas.

Functionalism and Higher Education

The field of international studies suffers from a deep and all-pervasive fragmentation that superficially makes for intellectual diversity and vitality. In fact, this diversity creates scattered armed camps that face one another across countless battlefields, but seldom if ever recognize one another or communicate. The logistics and material of the struggle are too familiar to escape detection: a well-endowed center, a prestigious-appearing letterhead, a journal vigorously promoted, and a band of devoted but often closed-minded disciples. Other less constant factors are the centers' leadership patterns, influence on policy, and scholarly and intellectual commitments. Some centers honor a single scholar; others reflect the interests of a tight-knit group, with no one scholar emerging as *primus inter pares*. Some are committed to influencing public policy whether at the United Nations or in American foreign policy. Others show little desire to shape policy options, but labor to uncover underlying philosophies and approaches. Finally, the nature of the commitment of the participants in such centers varies—some seeing themselves as little State or Defense Departments in exile, dedicated above all to becoming GHQ's on foreign policy studies, whereas others are no less committed to pure theory, whether behaviorally, philosophically, or historically oriented.

Viewed in this context, the British political theorist, the late David Mitrany, has staked out his own unusual position in the literature of international relations. His standing is unlike that of most prominent names in the field. He was never the denizen of a major professorial chair in a British or American university, though he was recognized through a distinguished appointment by the Princeton Institute of Advanced Studies. Until rather late in life he did not attract even a modest academic following, although serious scholars belatedly and rather unashamedly came to use his writings as a point of departure. Thus well-known political scientists were more likely to describe themselves as neofunctionalists or integrationists than as functionalists, which was Mitrany's term.

Mitrany's roots were not found in a single philosophical position or professional discipline. He drew his inspiration from liberalism, radicalism, syndicalism, Fabian socialism, nineteenth-century rationalism, the mixed economy, and New Deal experiments such as the TVA. He was a wartime intelligence researcher, a journalist, and foreign correspondent, a postwar planner, a seminar-and-discussion-group leader, a political advisor to a powerful international business concern, and a fairly traditional political theorist. He never headed a research center, he was without a generation or more of formal students, and he didn't found a scholarly or popular journal. Yet his influence has been far-reaching.

The reason for Mitrany's influence is not readily apparent. Seeking an explanation, one might ask what it was that caused Reinhold Niebuhr to describe Mitrany's founding study, *A Working Peace System*, as "the best I have seen on the subject" or Hans J. Morgenthau to assert that "the future of the civilized world is intimately tied to the functional approach to international organization."[1] Why should the *Times Literary Supplement* proclaim in July, 1974, that "if Functionalism does not work no other approach will." What is it about the outlook of functionalism that has challenged the interests and talents of scholars and observers of widely divergent viewpoints and methods? An inquiry into its contributions, limitations, and the problems it evokes may answer this question.

Functionalism's contribution to international thought is at least threefold: 1) It provides a useful framework for viewing efforts at international cooperation in rudimentary social and economic areas; 2) It offers a plausible approach to problems of world order and to bridging the gulf between international anarchy and world community; and 3) It adds a new dimension to international thinking traditionally confined to political, diplomatic, and legal questions. Functionalism's limitations as a rational and coherent theory arise not so much from these valid contributions as from its utopian, antipolitical, and noninstitutional character—limitations reflecting positive points of emphasis that nevertheless are imperiled by their excesses. Functionalism's problems derive from its failures with respect to historical prediction, its disparagement of ideas, and its lack of intellectual and scientific rigor—failures in no way unique to functionalism but nonetheless damaging to its historical and theoretical integrity.

It will not do to praise functionalism and ignore its limitations and the problems arising from them, any more than criticism of functionalism justifies overlooking the valid and significant role it plays in international studies. The intent of this discussion is to examine functionalism's relevance to higher education for development, alongside its limitations, and to explore a few of the general principles and conclusions that grow out of such a review. The findings on higher education stem from a twelve-donor agency study of higher education for development in Africa, Asia, and Latin

61

America. The agencies included the World Bank, Inter-American Development Bank, UNESCO, the United Nations Development Program (UNDP), UNICEF, United States Agency for International Development (USAID), the French Ministry of Foreign Affairs, the British Overseas Development Administration (ODA), the Canadian International Development Agency (CIDA), Canada's International Development Research Centre (IDRC), and the Ford and Rockefeller foundations.

Fieldwork in the study was conducted by three regional teams made up of African, Asian, and Latin American educators. The teams were headed by Aklilu Habte, then minister of youth and culture of Ethiopia, now head of the educational division of the World Bank and formerly president of the National University of Ethiopia; Puey Ungphakorn, until recently rector of Thammasat University in Bangkok, Thailand; and Alfonso Ocampo, former minister of health in Colombia and rector of Universidad del Valle in Cali, Colombia. Together these groups undertook twenty-three case studies, looking for important experiments in which higher education provided significant responses to urgent development needs such as increased food production, public health services, educational and cultural development, and population control. The case studies and the conclusions reached were published in 1976 and 1977 by Praeger in a two-volume work entitled *Higher Education and Social Change* by Kenneth W. Thompson and Barbara Fogel. (These themes are also discussed in my book, *Foreign Assistance: A View from the Private Sector.*)

1. CONTRIBUTIONS The first question worthy of attention is: Of what value is functionalism and what contribution does it make to understanding an inquiry into international education and its findings? Subordinate to this are the questions: Does functionalism provide a useful framework of thought for thus approaching international education? Does it offer a new perspective for education and world order? Does it add a new theoretical dimension? Because the guidelines of the twelve donor agencies placed emphasis on various national educational experiments, functionalism must be examined

within well-defined boundaries and not considered on a global basis. Notwithstanding, it is possible to offer some tentative impressions on the relevance of functionalism that deserve further discussion and study. As an intellectual framework, functionalism comes closer to fitting the problem area being considered than does any alternative framework. In one sense, it achieves its usefulness by default. Political realism is too much concerned with power and statecraft to be directly relevant on any overall basis. Idealism, which advocates that global solutions be undertaken immediately, bears little relation to what the developing countries are now seeking in higher education. Most importantly, education, though it has its political, legal, and diplomatic aspects, is a social and, increasingly, an economic enterprise. Among theories propounded, only functionalism deals with such a trend. Its controlling assumptions are therefore closer to the problems of higher education than is any competing theoretical approach.

It must also be recognized that the quest for world order in education is more likely to be achieved through the efforts of national educators working steadfastly on common problems than through ambitious theorizing on global education. Repeatedly, educators serving on regional teams queried other regions on new approaches to such fundamental issues as improved health delivery systems or increased food production. The Africans wanted to know more about the health sciences in general or about Candelaria (an experimental program for health care for the poor) in Cali, Colombia. Latin Americans, in turn, wondered about subprofessional training in engineering, accounting, and technical training at the Ngee Ann Technical College in Singapore, one of the few educational institutions anywhere that voluntarily downgraded itself from degree-granting to certificate-granting status in response to manpower planning needs. The Asians, for their part, asked about the use of artisans and technicians from the community in such institutions in Africa as Ahmadu Bello University in northern Nigeria and the University of Science and Technology in Ghana. Whether political theorists concerned with the nation-state know it or not, there is an emerging international community of scientists and educators who share common

63

concerns and are grappling with similar if not identical problems. Many such scientists and educators have taken their inspiration from and legitimized their experiments through Western experience and institutions. But these practices are becoming a thing of the past. For the future, these thinkers are turning more to one another's programs, especially as these relate to urgent Third World problems.

Finally, functionalism's most positive contribution may be in offering a striking new dimension to international thinking. Education has played a subordinate role in most of the writing on war and diplomacy. For the scholars of war and peace, the reigning question has been how effectively education has created a stronger sense of nationalism or alternatively a true world outlook. The UNESCO project on national histories is illustrative of this concern. Functionalism, by contrast, views education as a sectoral problem addressing itself to specific issues and defined areas, an approach that comes much closer to the dominant outlook in higher education study. It would be farfetched, I believe, to insist that the agronomists, physicians, and educators who studied or were the focus of study in the higher education project were primarily interested in nationalism or globalism as such. Given the urgency of the needs they sought to meet within relatively poor and hard-pressed countries or societies (an exception such as Singapore notwithstanding), they were unlikely to have written or thought much about the broader issues that have been the main concern of political scientists and lawyers. They key question is whether a functional interest in education promotes a spirit of internationalism in actions and programs.

2. LIMITATIONS Functionalism's limitations, I have suggested, stem from its utopian, antipolitical, and noninstitutional character. Its utopianism stems from a belief that successful functional cooperation will spill over into political and legal areas, gradually eroding the tenacious hold that national sovereignty has exerted on diplomats and statesmen. On one rather modest level, some evidence for this can be derived from the aforementioned study. Regional team members brought ministers and national development specialists into at least some of their discussions. Their findings suggest that

narrow nationalism is an obstacle to strong educational development within the smaller developing countries. Without exception, the regional teams called for more international exchange and heralded the value for education of foreign technical assistance.

At the same time, however, especially on the question of importing overall educational solutions, all three regional teams expressed skepticism and concern. Too often, outside experts came to lecture, not listen. The larger technical assistance agencies have a tendency to "package" the prevailing educational approach as the single answer to unique and particular problems. If the Third World was ever prepared to accept "Made in the United States" or "Made in Great Britain" as answers to their problems, that day has now passed.

Furthermore, the men and the processes set loose in facing local community problems tend, to the degree that they are successful, to heighten national pride and a sense of national identity. The Cameroon, with one of the most successful centers in the health sciences in Yaoundé, sees that center as a dramatically successful national effort, not one that lessens the force of the government of the Cameroon. Indeed the loyalty and commitment of national governments in general may well be the foremost ingredient required for a good educational recipe. If functionalism assumes an inevitable spillover from educational internationalism to political internationalism, UNESCO's failure to draw together ministers of education even to discuss successful educational experiments objectively, without constant reference to national pride, punctures that utopian balloon of functionalism.

The second limitation of functionalism reinforces this trend. It assumes that national and international politics will become less important as nonpolitical cooperation proceeds apace. Once again, the higher education study tends not to support this thesis. Governments in the developing countries see education as unmistakably political. They maintain that educational theories which presuppose a separation of government and universities are Western ideas, not applicable to meeting the desperate needs of poorer countries. In Tanzania ministers and government officials constitute 37 percent of the governing board of the University at Dar es Salaam. In Mali the so-called university is comprised of a series of institutes stemming from and dependent on such important ministries as agriculture, education, and the interior. The Ngee Ann Technical College in Singapore trains only the precise number of technicians called for by government planners. At least in the developing countries, it is simply not the case that a functional enterprise such as education leads to an erosion of national sovereignty. Quite the contrary is true.

Functionalism is a victim of yet another limitation. It has little to say about institutions and their comparability and interaction across national boundaries. "Function determines form" is functionalism's mandate. Pushed to an extreme, every unique function for every unique national problem will require a unique institutional form. Not only is this approach in conflict with the aims of organizational theory to achieve certain generalizable views about institutions. It also, in the field of education, detracts from the concerns that educators seek to encompass within the study of comparative education. In the present study, it was found that national educational systems in the Third World were significantly influenced by their educational heritage, even when they were reacting to and revolting against it. It is simply not possible to discuss higher education in Africa without referring to the institutional legacy of the British, the French, or the Americans. Perhaps the functionalist's mandate should be reformulated as "function ought to determine form." In fact, however, historical antecedents make this relation between function and form impossible in many cases, and the way out for the functionalist may be to recognize that history has a way of causing shipwreck for almost every simplifying social theory.

All this is not to deny the value or usefulness of the functionalist perspective, but merely to warn the historian of some of its limitations as Jacob Burkhardt did in calling attention to the self-deception of the "grand simplifiers."

3. FAILURES Functionalism's failures are a result, I have suggested, of its shortcomings in historical prediction, its disparagement of ideas, and its lack of scientific and intellectual rigor. These failures,

it should be pointed out, are in no way its monopoly. They occur and recur with almost every important social viewpoint and theory.

The annals of history are strewn with man's failures to foresee historical developments. Few if any on-the-spot observers anticipated the French or Russian revolutions. Building on his observations of social experiments such as the New Deal, Mitrany foresaw similar experiments of a functional or regional type breaking down national loyalties in international affairs. Some viewed the specialized agencies of the United Nations as a giant step in this direction after World War II. What ever the value of lessons learned and the functions performed by these bodies, the net effect of much of their functioning has been to highlight national struggles and rivalries. In a similar way, functionalism in higher education has not led, generally speaking, to a diminution of national sympathies. In fairness, this criticism cannot be leveled at the worldwide network of international agriculture institutes, which came close to substantiating the functional prediction. However, the same cannot be said of higher education in East and West Africa whose institutions have, at least in the past, had greater contact with metropolitan countries than with one another. In some parts of Africa, the trend has been toward a devolution of educational functions, as with the substitution of national educational systems in Francophone Africa for education under one uniform French system. The breakup of the University of East Africa and the failure to achieve a federated system of higher education in Southern Africa and Central America are further evidences of the failure of the functionalist prediction.

Functionalism has to a certain extent cleared the air by showing that functional experience was more likely to bring international cooperation than were rhetoric and ideas. Yet as Max Lerner once wrote "Men have thoughts; ideas have men." There is a certain contradiction inherent in the functionalist's disparagement of ideas that divide more than they unite and in Mitrany's faith in the power of the functionalist creed. It may also be true that an important idea, such as the concept of a rural health service in medical education, may be as significant as the creation of readily accessible rural health clinics. A mystique as often surrounds an announced educational creed as it does an innovative educational experiment, and to ignore one while praising the other may be as great an error as is overstressing abstract educational ideas without furnishing practical examples.

Finally, functionalism comes under fire from those who say it doesn't possess sufficient scientific and intellectual rigor. It is an approach of the most general sort, not a well-tested and refined social theory. To a certain extent, this criticism comes through in the higher education survey reported in *Higher Education and Social Change*. It is relatively simple to conclude that education is a functional endeavor, but far more complex to show that so general an approach provides any meaningful guidance on what to do or what to expect from cooperative endeavors in health education, agricultural education, or the training of teachers. One has only to ask what functionalism tells us about rural health stations as distinct from regional or provincial hospitals, say, in Cameroon or Colombia, to recognize the problem. There is a certain impreciseness and remoteness from urgent problems within given sectors of higher education that may illustrate the questioning of its intellectual rigor. Functionalism is similar to a Kantian category empty of specific content and therefore hard to use in actual social and political circumstances. To this, the functionalist will no doubt answer that this is its strength and significance. The failure is one, nonetheless, that supporters and critics must recognize more fully and move to clarify before seeing functionalism as a utopia or panacea.

4. CONCLUSIONS   The test of a theory of international relations rests on its usefulness for more than one segment of social experience. Higher education in the developing countries falls, broadly speaking, within the overall sector that David Mitrany defines as social and economic. Yet the linkages between education and the political system are close; education touches some of the most sensitive areas of a nation's life: the loyalties of the young and the building of manpower capacity. It would be surprising if governments, especially in poorer countries, were prepared to trust vital educational

processes to others. The leader of Tanzania, Julius Nyerere, once told me when I asked about outside assistance to Tanzania's primary and secondary school system: "Unless I can provide for the education of our young people, my people will turn out my government and me."

Nevertheless, functionalism is at least as appropriate for interpreting international cooperation in higher education as is any other theory. It is true that higher educators, especially those with professional competence, do constitute an international community of scholars who find it relatively easy to work together, free of overwhelming political constraints. I had little or no difficulty locating two dozen educators in less-developed countries who were competent to join in the study of higher education for development. Their professional reputations were evident to anyone who had worked in the field; and it was clear that whatever the political differences among their respective countries, they would have few problems working together. Although each of them had had some success in drawing in ministers and government officials, thus illustrating on a limited scale the spillover of the will to cooperate from nonpolitical to political subjects, their effectiveness was owing to their being primarily educators rather than promoters of transnational values among decision-makers in government. Their work has provided object lessons for the less global-minded of their associates; and there can be no doubt that in their governments' inner councils, men like G. L. Monekosso in the Cameroon, Aklilu Habte in Ethiopia, and Ambassador Soedjatmoko in Indonesia have provided sources of inspiration for international cooperation. Although functionalism tends to put its major emphasis on the transforming power of new social and economic processes and forces, the role of unique individuals embodying new functional approaches may be equally important.

Further, it is clear that the more specific and well-defined are the problems in education, the greater are the prospects for the relevance of the functionalist approach. Agricultural development serves as a striking example, specifically regarding the need for research and training to increase food production. International institutes for agricultural research are at work in Mexico, Colombia, the Philippines,

India, Nigeria, and Kenya, each devoting resources and manpower to the search for new high-yield varieties of specific crops. To illustrate, the Philippines concentrates on rice, Mexico on corn and wheat, and India on semi-arid lands food production. Scientists drawn from many countries work side by side, with little thought to differences of national origin. Successful experiments lead to multinational agreements on diversified programs in research and training. Far from hampering progress, a broadly based international effort stimulates scientific development and dissemination of results. International governing boards set policy for the institutes on the basis of regional, not national, needs and priorities. Just as successful public health ventures in Africa, Asia, and Latin America helped pave the way for cooperation in international agriculture, these international institutes foster a spirit of working together that gives evidence of spreading to other fields. Third World leaders have so often been subjected to promises without performance—from the promoters of technical assistance—that cooperative programs which bring results lead to closely related endeavors. Success breeds success and a willingness to undertake new experiments within the broad spectrum of development.

Yet social and economic advancement proceeds along an extended time line, seldom if ever yielding to instant solutions. The success stories of the international agriculture institutes are rooted in a quarter century of progress in the Mexican Agriculture Program of the Rockefeller Foundation initiated in 1943. The conquest of tropical diseases by private and public international health agencies had its beginnings at the turn of the century. It will not do for functionalists to portray political advancement as painfully slow and social progress as immediate. Functional approaches offer no immediately visible payoffs; the side effects or unintended benefits may be as valuable and far-reaching as direct successes. Yet no one would deny that in certain social areas cooperation that had been thwarted by political allegiances has advanced apace in a functional context. The long-run effects of educational and scientific leaders grown accustomed to cooperative efforts, of regional or worldwide approaches and solutions in one area attracting notice in other areas, and the experience of international bodies or boards in shaping transnational policies all combine to encourage respect for the functional approach.

Having said all this, experience in higher education dictates certain caveats to the functionalist idea. Higher education, like education in general, is wider and broader than a single problem. Functionalism and its assumptions fit agricultural education, specifically education and research for the increasing of food production. But higher education spans a far broader band of public policy, touching sensitive issues of national interest and class and society.

Beyond the widening circles and ramifications of its coming in contact with political and economic interests, higher education is closely linked with government, especially in the Third World. Therefore, successful experiments in higher education involving international cooperation tend as often to reinforce as to reduce nationalism. National governments with hard decisions to make about the allocation of scarce resources reserve to themselves decisions on education claim credit for any educational advances, and insist on a major role in the governance of universities. It is too much to expect that governments in less-developed countries will easily allow the control of higher education to pass to international bodies.

Finally, the higher education is influenced in every country by the cultural context of which it is a part. It is not a single commodity that can be packaged and delivered from one country to the next. In one country, institutes of higher education stem from and are dependent upon their respective ministries of government. In another country, separate educational institutions are expected to produce only those graduates for whom manpower-estimates forecast a need. In still other countries, the important role of independent institutions in liberal arts is slowly being recognized. To consider these several versions of higher education as falling within a single category is to prepare the way for misunderstanding and disillusionment.

What is common to each of these distinctions is their focus on the relation of higher education to government. In many industrialized countries, the two are considered independent; in Third World countries, they are part and parcel of the common national endeavor

of promoting national development and alleviating poverty. This
fact sets limits to functionalism's role, its importance notwithstanding. It in no way detracts from the benefits that may result from
international cooperation in higher education.

Functionalism
and Agriculture

Of all the areas of international cooperation that meet the tests of
functionalism, agriculture stands out. Not only does it offer an
example of early collaboration but such cooperation has continued
and expanded. It is possible to show that this has occurred because
agriculturalists working together are demonstrably engaged in a
functional endeavor. The evidence spans a broad area and includes
nearly a dozen areas of concern.

International agriculture involves the work not of political fig-
ures but of scientific and technical professionals. It starts with a
problem—world hunger—and moves forward in the social and economic realm. Its concerns are neither local nor regional. They are
worldwide, for feeding mankind and averting famine is an international need. The problem of hunger is universal.

The approach to this urgent need is one in which agricultural
scientists, wherever they may be, build on a tradition and established skills and techniques developed elsewhere in the world. For
example, various rice-growing techniques that were developed in
Louisiana and Japan have provided one basis for experimentation at
the International Rice Research Institute in the Philippines. Similarly, agronomists and plant pathologists who have worked on new
varieties and production techniques for corn and wheat in the Midwest have put this knowledge to work at the International Corn and
Wheat Center in Mexico. Since what has been learned in one area
cannot be applied without modification in another, a significant
amount of adaptation and modification is needed: research on
plant-breeding, testing for disease resistance in different circumstances, and studying the characteristics of individual varieties in
relation to local tastes and cultural preferences.

Food production, then, is aimed at meeting a primary, not a secondary need. The activities of professionals working on improved food production can proceed with some degree of freedom from politics and governmental pressures. It is possible to see agriculture as a technical and an applied scientific activity, less subject than other types of international cooperation to politics and hence to the dictates of national sovereignty. It can also be shown that cooperative programs in agriculture, much as has been the case with medicine and public health, can pave the way for international programs in other fields, such as education.

At the same time, it would be claiming too much to find in the history of international agricultural programs unmistakable signs of what Mitrany called the spillover effect. It is not true that national agricultural scientists working together on common problems have been able to persuade their political masters that national interests should be set aside. Nor can one point to instances in which national sovereignty has been eroded. The problem that has confounded every other attempt at limiting the absolute authority of the sovereign nation-state has not been solved by international cooperation in agriculture.

1. AGRICULTURE AS A SUCCESS STORY Notwithstanding its failure to change the patterns of political organization in the world, agricultural enterprise, both nationally and internationally, has been a functionalist success story. It concerns a field of technical assistance in which the donor agencies have something to give the poorer nations. Agricultural accomplishments in the developed countries are relevant, at least in broad terms, to the needs of the world community. This is particularly true of American agriculture in its various manifestations.

In part the success of American agriculture can be attributed to the land-grant colleges, which represent the most significant educational innovation in the United States in the nineteenth century. A group of English academics described them as "places where men are taught to throw manure about and act as wet nurses to steam engines." The Morrill Act in 1862 established a new system of

higher education. Whereas the distinguished universities of the East
had dominated the American educational scene and provided the
example of institutions capable of producing broadly educated men,
the land-grant institutions put their stress on the practical—the
applied sciences and arts. Universities destined to become large-
scale educational centers appeared out of nowhere. A chicken farmer
in Michigan brought a new institution, Michigan State, from the
position of a rather small and provincial university to one of national
and international prominence. What John Hannah accomplished in
East Lansing, Michigan, had earlier occurred at Cornell, Minnesota,
and Wisconsin.

What are the principal characteristics of the land-grant university
as it has developed throughout the United States? In the first place, it
has been more vocationally oriented than have Ivy League universities and their counterparts. The links between study and work are
closer than in other universities. Education is tied to the labor mar-
ket within the region and the nation. Students of education point out
that this emphasis means that enrollments remain stable or significantly increase when declines occur in more traditional liberal arts
institutions because of the decrease in job opportunities for arts and
sciences graduates.

Second, the curriculum and programs of land-grant institutions
are geared to local needs and problems. Some of the great private
universities located in large metropolitan areas pride themselves on
being *in* but not *of* their cities. It is said that Harvard University
contributes little in political and economic leadership to Cambridge.
The same has been true in recent years of the University of Chicago,
though men like Julian Levi, brother of former president, Edward
Levi, have played a decisive role in neighborhood redevelopment.
The educational philosophy of land-grant institutions is the direct
opposite. These colleges and universities pride themselves on taking a direct and continuing interest in the problems of their communities. If their problem-solving emphasis directed at the needs of
their immediate localities has somewhat diminished or been redi-
rected to nationwide problems as they have grown in size and scope,
their underlying philosophy remains intact.

Third, land-grant institutions have designed and carried out programs involving a substantial degree of adaptation and extension of the university's work and outreach. Examples include programs for the training of county agents and short courses and summer programs in agriculture. My father, who lived out his youth in a rural area near Madison, Wisconsin, and other members of his family spent three or four weeks each summer at the University of Wisconsin learning new and improved approaches to agricultural production. Such universities as Wisconsin, Minnesota, and Cornell also developed radio and publication programs to aid the farmer, even issuing leaflets and brochures written in simple, nonscientific language and applicable to local circumstances.

Fourth, land-grant institutions were in the forefront of educational centers that brought education to the people. Branches of major state universities were established in other parts of the state, and, carrying the land-grant philosophy another step, these branches geared their offerings to whatever needs were more pressing within each particular locality.

Fifth, it was early recognized that educational institutions in the twentieth century must think in terms of lifelong learning. In this the land-grant institutions anticipated an educational viewpoint that came into prominence in the 1960s with a widely discussed report by UNESCO on the need for continuing education of adults as well as young people. It is obvious that the industrialized and nonindustrialized countries respond to this need in the light of different problems and circumstances. In the industrial countries, the growing mechanization of work and life has driven many adults to seek human satisfaction and self-realization outside their day-to-day employment; they are turning in ever larger numbers to continuing education and community college programs. Liberated from long hours of drudgery by shorter work weeks, they are seeking renewal in the offerings of adult education. In the less-developed countries, economic pressures and trained manpower shortages, rather than increased leisure, have brought adults into educational institutions. So-called mature student programs are now an established part of educational opportunities in most African universities. If one were to look for the sources of these educational innovations, many of them go back to concepts of the land-grant college movement.

Sixth, land-grant education, in common with the theory of functionalism, begins with an urgent problem. The core precept is the belief that the main business of education is to prepare men and women to cope with the amelioration of difficult and pressing circumstances. Its approach in this respect is inductive, not deductive. The starting point is not a general principle, but a problem for which education is assumed to have a contribution to make.

Seventh, the leadership of land-grant institutions, it follows, is composed not so much of educational philosophers as of technical professionals. They constitute a network of experts rotating in and out of positions of power in the public and private sectors. One example can be drawn from the field of agriculture. An extraordinarily capable group of scientists are the agriculturalists who have served as leaders of the land-grant institutions, men like Clifford Hardin, Earl Butz, James Jensen, Louis Morrill, Clifton R. Wharton, Jr., and John Hannah, who later served as secretaries of agriculture or leaders of technical assistance programs. These men constitute an educational and scientific elite, apart from the foreign policy establishment. They have been trustees and advisors to foundations and government agencies that have provided agricultural assistance to the less-developed countries. They are known in these countries as trusted friends and consultants who have played an important role in the shaping of agricultural education and policy.

Eighth, the land-grant institutions in the United States have emerged as important clearinghouses and repositories of agricultural know-how and information. They are centers in which new varieties of basic food crops have been developed, and their leaders are always willing to share their findings and their expertise with international agricultural institutes and ministries of agriculture in other countries.

Ninth, the most distinctive characteristic of the land-grant institutions is their emphasis on service. There is widespread agreement that the threefold task of those in higher education is to teach, to engage in research, and to render service. Different educational institutions have emphasized these functions in varying degrees. The great private institutions such as Harvard, MIT, and Stanford have won fame and renown as research institutions. Although land-grant institutions have not neglected research in certain applied scientific areas, their greatest contribution has been the service they provide to agencies of government and to private corporations. A tradition of service has grown up that enables at least some of these institutions to make their best scholars and scientists available to developing countries for extended periods of residence and for the training of indigenous leaders. It is increasingly common for such institutions to grant academic leaves to their strongest faculty members for three or four years of service abroad, much as strong research universities grant similar research leaves to their most outstanding basic scientists. For example, a well-known agricultural economist from the University of Minnesota has over the past dozen years been a regular faculty member of Kasetsart University in Bangkok, Thailand, while retaining his professorship at Minnesota. Some land-grant universities have in effect two faculties in certain fields, one for teaching and research at home and the other for similar work abroad. Thus these institutions include in their budgets provision for a cadre of professors engaged in international service. Moreover, the land-grant colleges have taken the lead in initiating sister-university relations with institutions in the Third World. Their willingness to undertake such missions can only reflect their commitment to service.

The special problems of the less-developed countries and their most urgent needs and priorities have made the land-grant pattern congenial to the thinking of their leaders. But even for those whose educational formation and background falls within non-American-developed educational systems, the land-grant system is attractive. Sir Eric Ashby (now Lord Ashby) of Clare College, Oxford University, in England, was the author of a major review of higher education in Nigeria following that country's independence. Sir Eric urged Nigerians, and donor agencies that might assist them, to revise the inherited educational system that was patterned after the University of London and kept a continuing special relation with that institution. The Ashby Commission asked if the land-grant institution was not more relevant to local needs in Nigeria. Members of the commission proposed a series of new universities in Nigeria, providing clear educational alternatives to the Ox-bridge model; and shortly thereafter a new university based on these proposals was created in the eastern region at Nssuka, with a special relation to Michigan State University.

Although it is still too early to measure the results of these changing educational patterns in Nigeria, it is significant that the other new universities there—especially at Ife near Ibadan and in Zaria in northern Nigeria (Ahmadu Bello University)—have patterned themselves more after the American land-grant university than after the British model. Slavish imitation of any outside model is risky, and the Nigerians and other African educators have struggled to avoid this mistake. It is also true that the existence of such alternative educational systems has influenced and led to change in a more traditional British institution such as Ibadan University. The African experience teaches that the existence of these alternatives and more serious attention to problems in the agricultural and nonagricultural faculties has had a constructive effect.

2. THE CAPACITY OF AMERICAN AGRICULTURE VIEWED IN FUNCTIONAL TERMS The success story of American agriculture and the unique strengths of the land-grant college movement provide only a partial explanation of the capacity of American agriculture. Its resources are also a result of its heritage—the quality and vitality of its leaders, its curious intermingling of individualism and communalism, its blending of parochialism and universalism.

The heritage of American agriculture stems from its noteworthy achievements in opening a vast continent to settlement and feeding an expanding population. Many of the nation's first immigrants arrived in the new land from western and northern Europe where they had farmed the land, raised livestock, and experimented agriculturally. As the early settlers moved westward they looked for a terrain of rivers and plains such as they knew in Europe. Ole Rolvaag and Herbert Krause, respectively, in *Giants in the Earth* and *Wind With-*

out *Rain*, have written of the suffering and adversity, the courage and inventiveness of the Scandinavian immigrants. Later waves of migration brought workers and technicians from southern and eastern Europe. Because those who made up the agricultural stratum were so resourceful, the specter of hunger and famine that has threatened other societies was not as forbidding to the new Americans. To credit the skills of the American farmer is not to minimize the advantages of the abundant productivity of the soil or of an equable climate and rainfall.

The triumphs of the American farmer in conquering the wilderness and his survival against great odds produced a new breed of fearless and outspoken leaders whose thinking and attitudes were rooted in local needs and circumstances. Social and political movements such as populism, the Farm Labor party, and the Progressive party drew on the drive, ambition, and discontent of these men. They were symbols of the sturdy individualism and stubborn persistence in the face of ever-changing conditions of winds and weather. At the same time, they spoke out against early injustices and exploitation by the railroads, utilities, and a government that was remote and indifferent to their needs and problems. Less polished and urbane than business and industrial leaders, the nation's agricultural leaders were blunt and plainspoken, wary of domination by the favored few of an eastern elite.

Yet individualism alone is not adequate to describe rural motivation. When disaster struck, it was the whole community that helped raise homes or barns that had been destroyed—and then celebrated with revelry and dance what people joining together had accomplished. Individualism and communalism coexisted in practice, however much they conflicted in theory and logic. Because men had learned to help themselves, they were better able to help others. Service had its birth in these early community beginnings; and it comes as no surprise, therefore, that individuals in the rural sector were responsive in the mid-twentieth century to calls for help from abroad.

Finally, paradoxical as it may seem given its motivation to serve mankind, no group in American life has been, from a certain standpoint, more parochial. It is the American farmer who, until recent decades at least, has protested the acts of faraway government, resisted cries for help by the cities, and questioned internationalism whatever its creedal or political formulations. Rural areas have cradled isolationalism, welcomed opposition groups such as America First, nurtured xenophobia, and doubted the value of any foreign involvements. Whatever the motivating force, whether it has been fear and resentment of the rich and powerful or the Jeffersonian belief that it was impossible to find human virtue outside of small cities and rural areas, agricultural America has affirmed loyalty to what was local and immediate and questioned cosmopolitanism and internationalism as leading to an effete way of life.

Yet rural peoples have also clung to a dream that was universal, a belief that the good life was rooted in religion, hard work, and the family. Men who lived close to the soil were assumed to have integrity and moral stamina, whether they happened to be in Iowa or Nigeria. Their religious heritage had bound them together in the Christian missionary movement, and it was not too farfetched for American agronomists or plant pathologists to see continuity between their missionary forefathers and themselves as they worked in a secular and scientific world. Religious precepts taught that all men were brothers. Mankind everywhere had both spiritual and material needs to which the privileged few were duty bound to contribute. It was not surprising, therefore, that despite a certain strain of parochialism, rural America rose to the challenge of helping feed the world. Such universalism was linked to the simple and rudimentary aspects of life even as farm people continued to look with distaste and suspicion on clever international diplomacy or high-flown language concerning world power and national interests.

Taken together, these four factors—the heritage of rural America, the energy and convictions of its leaders, its intermingling of individualism and communalism, and its blending of parochialism and universality—combined to give American agriculturalists a unique capacity in functional terms. Here was an identifiable group with a mission of its own, willing and able to contribute to the world not as nations had traditionally assisted one another through arms and

trade but through people working together for agricultural development. American agricultural scientists were carried along in their
mission by the conviction that they could work not necessarily with
Nigerians in general or with any other nationality but with Nigerian
agriculturalists. Despite the parochialism that pervaded some of
their thinking, they were internationalists in the sense that they had
confidence that their capacity in agriculture was relevant to what
they called the conquest of hunger everywhere. American agriculture had fed a growing population, and those primarily responsible
were convinced they could help others to revolutionize agricultural
productivity, to turn their systems around and feed their own people
through strategies of self-help. This wider task required not the usual
patterns of emergency food aid, but new forms of functional cooperation on which American specialists would stake their prestige.

Agricultural cooperation across national boundaries aimed at
assisting Third World countries represents a particular kind of functionalism. It is much closer to what some have called "developmental functionalism," which is aimed at assisting the growth of
less-developed countries. It contrasts with what Mitrany and others
have denominated "regulatory functionalism," or the building of
larger units of cooperating groups within a region or the world. The
latter type of functionalism has been the pattern of social and economic cooperation within the industrial world.

One other distinction deserves mention. Agricultural cooperation, as described here, begins from an American base. Its core is
American agricultural know-how. However, as agriculturalists en-
visage the effort, its ultimate goal is to assist the "well-being of
mankind." It is grounded in agriculturalists working with agriculturalists regardless of national origin. For this reason, and particularly because the initiative in the 1950s and 1960s came from private
organizations, it is an experiment in functionalism, not one aspect of
American foreign policy.

3. THE INTERNATIONALIZATION OF AGRICULTURE That the improvement of agriculture is viewed as a worldwide mission is in part a
result of the strength and capacity of American agriculture, reflected

in the land-grant college movement, and in part a result of the desperate straits of the poorer nations struggling to feed themselves. American efforts to help other peoples began with private and public efforts in emergency and rescue operations. When disaster struck, whether in catastrophes of nature or in unremitting famines, Americans were among the first to respond. Church groups and other humanitarian agencies rallied to deliver food and other forms of relief. The Food for Peace program of the government is only the most recent large-scale attempt to help the starving and the homeless. The practice of needy people's turning to America testifies both to our recognized humanitarianism and to the successes of American agriculture. Negatively, it demonstrates a sense of dissatisfaction with the failures of other agricultural approaches, whether the Russian attempt to feed the peoples of the Soviet Union or the less-than-spectacular success of the French and the British in Africa and Asia.

The American approach to feeding the world represents the convergence of a missionary spirit of a people and of a felt need expressed particularly by the governmental leaders and educators of Africa and Asia. I learned this in numerous conversations from the late 1950s to early 1970s as the coordinator of international programs for the Rockefeller Foundation. By the 1960s African leaders in particular were growing restive with existing assistance programs. As already noted, the Ashby Commission called for another type of education in Africa. The late Sir Alexander Carr-Saunders, a renowned British demographer and social scientist, headed several survey teams that made similar recommendations to various universities founded by the British in Africa. Asians expressed concern with the high price of the brain drain, as national educators trained abroad were attracted by institutions outside their own countries. Asian and African universities whose agriculture programs had enjoyed at best limited success under British, French, and German tutelage requested American technical assistance. Several institutions, including Makerere College in Uganda and Asian universities in India and Indonesia, went so far as appointing American agricultural educators with land-grant college backgrounds as deans of their agriculture faculties. Ralph W. Cummings, director of the Rockefeller Foundation's agriculture program in India who later headed the International Institute on Arid Lands Agriculture Research in Hydrabad (ICRISAT), promoted the development of seven agricultural universities in India, all modeled after the land-grant universities. Indonesia turned to the Rockefeller and Ford foundations for the strengthening of its agricultural institutes and universities. The University of the Philippines reorganized its system of agricultural education with help from Cornell University, the International Rice Research Institute (IRRI), and the Ford Foundation. Kasetsart University in Thailand drew heavily on the agriculture staff of the Rockefeller Foundation and several land-grant universities. Zaire, Tanzania, Ethiopia, and Kenya in Africa made similar calls on professional agriculturalists from the United States. Indeed, it is difficult to think of a major country in Africa and Asia that has not been touched by American agriculture, bringing to fruition the internationalization of this nation's effort to be helpful not only in these continents but in Latin America as well.

4. THE COMMON EMPHASIS OF THE AMERICAN AGRICULTURAL EFFORT ABROAD How can we account for the spread of American agricultural ideas and practices? What have been the working principles and the common emphases of the effort? What explains its widespread influence throughout the developing world? There are at least eight distinguishing characteristics of the approach that strengthen and reinforce one another.

First, American agricultural scientists at work in the Third World have given the highest priority to improved agricultural production, not to research for research's sake. Other traditions, and in particular the British, had laid greater stress on a form of agricultural education aimed at training broadly educated agriculturalists. As one traveled by airplane in the 1960s from London to universities in West or East Africa, it was rare not to meet British-trained agriculturalists who could recite the history and culture of every major crop in Africa. At early morning refueling stops en route to their destination, these remarkably cultured men put Americans to shame with their encyclopedic knowledge of the origins and development of plants and animals across the continent, many introduced or cultivated by the colonial power. What was missing, however, was the passionate concern of American agronomists or plant pathologists for expanding and diversifying agricultural production in order to eliminate the hunger of the people of the country or region, a lack some Englishmen were frank to admit to their American friends in moments of candor. It was this passionate concern that inspired American agriculturalists to work long hours side by side with agriculturalists of other nations, without ever asking who would receive the credit for their functional endeavor. Anyone who looked in on the agricultural research institutes left with a sense that here were men laboring with a "grand obsession."

Second, the Americans had one all-consuming objective, if not obsession, in their blueprints for agricultural universities. It was essential that experiment stations be established for practical work within these institutions. Many Asian and African universities lacked such a facility, putting more stress on the theory than on the practice of agriculture. Americans insisted there must be a place where fledgling agriculturalists "could learn to grow a crop."

Third, Americans maintained that there must be links with ministries of agriculture. Universities must not exist in isolation from the principal actors on the agricultural scene. The British had separated governmental research stations from educational institutions; but at least partially in response to American influence, these two parts of the agricultural system were joined when the newer universities came into being as with the new university in Northern Nigeria, Ahmadu Bello. When the Rockefeller Foundation agreed to help the agricultural faculty at Gadja Mada University in Jojakarta, Indonesia, it did so on condition that various plots of land at some distance from the university be joined together in an experiment station with links to the ministry of agriculture.

Fourth, the American approach also laid stress on the building of substantial storage and retrieval systems. It was essential, the Americans argued, that a vast array of plant varieties be brought together in one place readily accessible to agricultural researchers.

Corn and wheat banks were established at almost every center in which work was undertaken. This was also done for potatoes, sorghum, and beans, as well as indigenous crops with which Americans had little initial familiarity.

Fifth, Americans insisted that trainees put on overalls and go out into the field. Book learning was not enough. The Rockefeller Foundation staff, when it went into Mexico in 1943, found that young Mexicans had imagined they were to be trained for desk jobs. Their resistance to soiling their hands was overcome, however, when they found their American colleagues spent most of their working hours teaching themselves and their students "how to plant a crop of wheat in Mexico." Nobel Prize winner Norman Borlaug set an example by working from sunup to sundown in the wheat fields of northern Mexico, and his example proved contagious.

Sixth, another point of doctrine emphasized the integration of training and research. Although the American team of the Rockefeller Foundation in Mexico began its work within the so-called Office of Special Studies within the Ministry of Agriculture, it quickly turned its attention to the creation of its first-class Graduate School of Agriculture at Chapingo. There the emphasis, as in the land-grant colleges, was on training for agricultural production, not on agricultural theory.

Seventh, it was also taken as given that what was learned in one place in agricultural sciences had relevance for other places. Widespread exchange of information and materials and, wherever possible, of trained personnel, was encouraged. Nor were the learners to be exempt from such exchange, for it was assumed from the beginning that Mexicans, for example, had a responsibility to share information and know-how with agriculturalists in Central America.

Eighth, the overall activity of building agricultural capacity and its success was dependent upon the existence of highly qualified professionals who had something to contribute to colleagues in other countries. A career service was established by organizations such as the Rockefeller Foundation and by the land-grant institutions financed from private and public sources. The concept of a career service reached its culmination in the establishment in 1975 of an International Agricultural Development Service (IADS), composed of agricultural personnel who had had experience in one or more developing countries and were available for service elsewhere.

5. REINFORCING PROGRAMS The approach of the land-grant institutions was strengthened and reinforced by what were called country programs brought into being by agencies such as the Rockefeller Foundation. In 1943 that organization, after careful study and review, launched its first country program in agricultural research and training in Mexico and followed this, as we have seen (pp. 70, 82–83, 84–86, 87; see also pp. 100–102), by establishing successive programs in Colombia (1950), Chile (1953), the Philippines (1959), India (1960), and Nigeria (1962). Not only did these programs call on the resources of skilled professionals from land-grant institutions, they also helped such scientists and technicians to develop an identity, an *esprit de corps.* The leaders of the programs developed pride in their own approach and a mild skepticism with the fixed concepts of the land-grant approach. They constituted small, close-knit bodies of professionals who never doubted their ability to so alter the agricultural production systems of the countries in which they worked as to move from a crop-deficit to crop-surplus position. So single-minded was their commitment that I found them hesitant to explore broader issues of agricultural economics, agricultural policy, and land reform. Through their efforts, Mexico was able to terminate the importation of corn and wheat, thereby protecting scarce foreign-exchange reserves.

Success in the country programs led to larger regional efforts and to the creation of international agriculture institutes manned by experienced leaders from the country programs who followed the example set by the International Health Division of the Rockefeller Foundation, as well as other medicine and public health agencies. Their aim was to keep intact the human capital developed by the country program and make it available on a wider geographical basis.

Finally, a coalition of some twenty-five or thirty donor agencies—private and public—joined in the 1960s to form a consortium of policy and fund-raising bodies constituting the Consultative Group on International Agricultural Research. The efforts of this group assured that the necessary support for the continuation of a wide range of cooperative activities in agricultural research and training in the developing countries would be forthcoming.

6. THE WORLD FOOD CONFERENCE AND THE WORLD FOOD COUNCIL
The efforts made by these bodies and others that have marshaled the skills and talents of the international community of agricultural scientists were the prelude to a far larger effort in the 1970s to meet the problem of world hunger. In 1972 the World Food Conference was convened in Rome, bringing together representatives from both the developed and less-developed countries. The conference was an expression of the desire for a North/South dialogue; it represented the same type of producers' and consumers' conference that had been held in the energy field. Such a meeting was also a further sign of the equality of nations exemplified in the work of the United Nations and evidenced the fact that the existing international specialized agency in agriculture, the Food and Agriculture Organization (FAO), had left something to be desired. The World Food Conference, and the World Food Council it brought into being, represented the chance of carrying further the important effort begun in the 1940s to feed the world. From the standpoint of functionalism, it showed the organic growth from the small beginnings of a handful of agricultural scientists laboring to end the crop-deficit position of Mexico.

With the World Food Conference in Rome, the international agricultural effort moved across the threshold that separates a functional endeavor from one involving politics and the high governmental policies of nation-states. It engaged domestic political groups in every participating country. For example, the chief spokesmen for the United States on issues in contention were Secretaries Henry Kissinger and Earl Butz, if not President Ford, for a Republican administration, and Senators George McGovern and Hubert Humphrey for the Democrats. In international politics, it involved the clash of interest between the developed and the developing countries. Politicians, not agricultural scientists, moved to the center of the stage. It was no longer possible to describe international agricultural cooperation in primarily technical and economic terms. The issue that remains unresolved is whether the functional cooperation that prevailed from the 1940s to the end of the 1960s has been superseded by a political clash of interests or whether functionalism has worn away some of the extreme loyalties that dominated other sectors of international relations. Is it fair to ask whether the politicization of functionalism introduces the reverse effect of what David Mitrany forecast, namely a "spilling-over" of politics into economic and technical areas rather than the "spilling over" of functional cooperation into international politics?

7. CONCLUSIONS Agricultural cooperation on the international plane appears to fit many of the important criteria of functionalism. It begins with an urgent problem, it has a worldwide rather than a local or national character, and it engages the best efforts of well-trained technical professionals. Moreover, the building of agricultural capacity in at least some of the developing countries has shown an organic functional growth. It has moved from small beginnings by means of an international network of agricultural experts toward ameliorating if not solving the problem of world hunger. Governments, in accepting international agricultural assistance, have been willing to override narrow partisan and political interests. For example, Pakistan's agricultural development in the 1960s was undertaken against the advice of entrenched local agricultural leaders whose advice was set aside when President Ayub Khan accepted the counsel of Norman Borlaug and a group of outside agricultural experts. Some African and Asian universities have proven ready to go outside their own national leadership to bring in international leaders in such posts as deans of their major agricultural universities. The work of the international community of agricultural professionals far exceeds the weight of their numbers or their political influence, even within their own countries. They have been, as it were, mercenaries for peace and agricultural development, much as Swiss soldiers were mercenaries for war in another historical epoch. Known to each other, agricultural scientists have shared their knowl-

edge with one another and with peoples of less-advantaged countries, always paying more attention to human need and less to national boundaries.

Nevertheless, success in agricultural development has brought representatives of nation-states and the community of agricultural scientists to a level at which functionalist concepts no longer apply. Once decisions on world food production become a matter of high policy within states and engage its principal politicians, a new set of concerns come into play. Special interest groups have always watched over the work of agricultural scientists in international projects. The National Association of Wheat Growers and other agricultural pressure groups in the United States have never been particularly favorable to efforts at making Mexico self-sufficient in wheat production. However, more than special interest groups are involved when the United States participates in the World Food Council. Not subnational but national interests come into play. It would be asking too much of functional cooperation to expect that these would be set aside.

Further, the success of functionalism depends on playing down the role of ideological forces in international relations. Nations that adopt a crusading and messianic posture may score ideological points on one another, but they are unlikely to achieve full cooperation. This is the risk the community of nations runs in making agricultural cooperation depend on the resolution of the North/South conflict at the World Food Council. Ambassador Moynihan was right in pointing out that as the risk of military confrontation diminishes in the Cold War the prospect of ideological confrontation rises. If a similar increase in ideological confrontation occurs in relationships between the developed and less-developed countries, it could mean the end of functional cooperation.

Finally, the notion that food can be used as an instrument of foreign policy is in itself antithetical to functionalism. If this is the framework in which international agricultural cooperation is viewed, the prospects for any important achievement of functional cooperation will diminish or disappear. Rivalry and conflict are still the major patterns of relations among states, and unfortunately this

89

aspect of international relations is likely to prevail over international cooperation in agriculture if the more recent trends evident at the Rome conference and the World Food Council persist.

Functionalism
and Foundations

General-purpose foundations in the United States are predominantly a phenomenon of American life. There are approximately 26,500 such organizations with assets of $30 billion. They are nonprofit organizations, created under state or federal law to serve the common good. Their activities are made possible through privileges and immunities accorded by established tax laws. They enjoy freedom to innovate and a flexibility that public bodies subject to continuous scrutiny and committee hearings seldom know. The staff and chief executive officers of foundations are responsible to boards of trustees in whom there resides a public trust. Since 1969, however, foundations have operated under a revised tax law which imposes more constraints than had previously existed.

Private foundations in the United States meet many of the criteria set forth in the functionalist approach. They are nonpolitical, staffed by professionals, problem-centered, responsive to urgent community needs; some of them see their mission as worldwide, without reference to national boundaries. Their sphere of interest is social and economic and includes health and sanitation, agriculture and nutrition, and environment and culture. They foster international cooperation by bringing professionals together to attack a common problem and by mobilizing their skills and talents without asking what nationalities they represent. The goal of foundations, at least those whose activities go on outside their own countries, is to build networks of cooperative relations that bind peoples together. The work of general-purpose foundations with international concerns is transnational in character, not confined to a given locality and nation. In mode of operation, the foundations have tried to teach by building habits and attitudes of cooperation, without discussing such cooperation in the abstract or erecting theories about transnational cooperation. Indeed I have been impressed by the limited appeal of broad theories of international relations to the practitioners of foundations. The functionalists talk about the importance of attacking the problem of sovereignty indirectly and reducing its controlling influence by erosion rather than by substituting a powerful international authority for the sovereign state. I do not recall any foundation leaders with whom I have worked ever addressing themselves in any way to the issue. Such men are for the most part highly practical workers in fields such as agriculture or medicine, men who are seldom concerned with broader issues. This is particularly true if we turn to them for conclusions about their effect upon cooperative actions in political sectors, the so-called spillover effect, as functionalists have defined it. Notwithstanding, it cannot be denied that consequences flow from scientists working side by side on an urgent problem, whatever their national origins.

1. THE HISTORY OF FOUNDATIONS   The American foundation with broad purposes, functioning within and outside the nation's borders, had its origins in the first and second decades of the twentieth century. The cynics have said that foundations were the result of robber barons turning their efforts and some of their profits to charity. Strong individuals who had welded together mighty industrial empires through means that were, at best, morally ambiguous sought to reconstitute the family name and image and to perpetuate their influence. At the same time, first generation foundation leaders were not driven to seek fame through their philanthropy. They were men of immense self-confidence who were prepared to give independence and responsibility to professional staffs charged with the day-by-day operation of new organizations. There was less outright interference in the work of highly skilled scientists and qualified educators by the donor or his family than was to be true in a subsequent era.

The first foundations were born in an atmosphere of extreme public skepticism. Their founders' intentions were questioned, and there was debate by lawmakers regarding their enfranchisement. For some, it proved more feasible to establish the new organizations under state rather than federal charters. The earliest charters, much like the early state constitutions, established broad general mandates and left the details to responsible trustees and officers. Thus the Rockefeller Foundation was established to serve "the well-being of mankind" everywhere. It was assumed that foundations, in order to contribute to society's most urgent needs, required flexibility and the capacity to adapt to changing necessities and demands. The founders had the foresight to resist tying the work to the dead hand of the past.

The early foundations were international from the start, a characteristic that has been conspicuously missing in some of the later ones. The thinking of their founders was a blending of Christian and humanistic impulses. At one of the first meetings of the board of trustees of the Rockefeller Foundation, a spokesman for the extension of one of the health programs into other countries found his justification in the Biblical command, "Come over and help us in Macedonia." It was also a tenet of faith that reason applied to human problems would bring them under control and lead to their solution.

The giant foundations have come into being at several important periods in American history. The Carnegie Corporation and the Rockefeller Foundation were established early in the twentieth century. The Ford Foundation was a product of the post–World War II years, as were the Johnson Foundation and the greatly expanded Lilly Endowment and the Edna McConnell Clark Foundation. It is more difficult to associate some of these later philanthropies with functionalist theory, because they have been less committed to the idea of professionals allocating funds and participating actively in the scientific work that foundations had selected for emphasis. Yet most, in greater or less degree, pursue certain functionalist lines of activity.

2. THE FOUNDATIONS' MODE OF OPERATION The early foundations in particular recognized initially that their success depended on their following a functionalist approach. Their boards of trustees drew a clear line between policy determination and the execution of that policy. The province of the boards was to deliberate and choose a problem or series of problems to which the foundation staffs could

seek solutions. For some of the first American foundations, response to the problem of public health underlay the amelioration of every other problem. Even though private resources were never considered sufficient to solve such problems, the foundations assumed they could make a start. The concept of assisting through providing seed money had its origins at this time. Foundation leaders proceeded on the assumption that they could test an idea or approach through one or more pilot projects; if these proved successful, other funding agencies with greater resources would take over. Thus foundations from the beginning had links with local, state, and federal agencies that observed the pilot work, sometimes participating and eventually carrying it forward when a solid experimental base had been laid.

A second assumption fundamental to the foundations' mode of operation was that not the symptoms but the root cause of a problem should be the point of entry. Questions arose as to what these root causes were, and here the task of identification exceeded the competence of any single group of lay trustees. To assist at this level, the trustees and senior executives of the foundations recruited top educators and scientists. The closest links were maintained with universities, medical schools, and schools of public health. The foundations were organized by professional divisions such as medicine, public health, and the social sciences; members of these divisions were granted a large measure of independence and freedom to conduct professional studies and investigations. The advantages that foundations enjoyed vis-à-vis political controls were carried forward in the autonomy of their staffs. Strong and respected individuals who gave first priority to their trusteeship and carried over few if any divided loyalties were watchdogs over the independence of their staffs. Trustees seldom tried to impose their private interests. As a result, an *esprit de corps* and self-respect grew up among staff members; this has not always been matched in the more recent past. Trustees were prepared in a field such as medicine to trust their professional staffs. A mystique of professional competence dominated their efforts. The papers and writings of these early scientists reflect a confidence and pride which has diminished as public images have come to replace results as the paramount criteria for measuring the foundations' work.

It should be noted that although these first efforts did not carry an antigovernment viewpoint, the early foundations reserved the right to be independent of government. Part of the sense of pride of the officers stemmed from the fact that staff members could act quickly to meet human needs and were less constrained to employ high-cost public relations techniques to justify themselves either to government or to a broad and undifferentiated public. There was less obsession with self-justification and the claiming of institutional credit, more concern with showing that other institutions and individuals to whom the foundations had given their funds and their confidence had produced significant work and achieved important scientific breakthroughs that also served the well-being of mankind.

Foundation representatives operated from "a packed suitcase." They came and went in their work, especially abroad, not from concern for their nation's foreign policy or the demands of international politics, but because there was a job to do. So long as they judged that they had a contribution to make, they continued their labors, subject only to the decision of scientific peers and superiors. They were largely free of the need to justify their efforts to nonscientific decision-makers. They were not victims of the quarterly, semiannual, or annual hearings of political bodies; their foreign assistance was seldom plagued by what has been called the problem of one-year appropriations and two-year budgets designed to meet twenty-year human needs.

Finally, these men and women sought answers both in national and international laboratories. They moved back and forth between American and foreign settings where the problem and the solution took on different forms and expressions. What was learned about infectious diseases in the United States was applied in Brazil and vice versa. The world was their laboratory; and they followed the problem in their search for medical and public health solutions that would serve not Americans alone but mankind.

3. SHIFTING PROGRAMS AND PROBLEMS The foundations have, for the most part, been free to shift their priorities. Their aim has been to

identify the single most urgent problem to which foundation resources and professional capacity could, with some prospect of success, be applied. Health was an early focal point in the work of the
Rockefeller Foundation and some of its related bodies such as the
International Sanitary Commission and the International Health Division. Poor health was identified as the primary scourge of mankind. A decision was made to proceed by concentrating on a few
specific diseases wherever they were major health problems: yellow
fever, yaws, hookworm, and malaria. The quest for remedies and
cures was one aspect of the approach. The other was improved
health care and better health delivery systems. The foundations were
instrumental in creating schools of public health. They pioneered in
new concepts and better and more relevant training. They sponsored
studies of medical education, the most famous resulting in the
Flexner Report, in which the distinguished medical scientist and
public health leader, Abraham Flexner, described existing medical
schools as made up of "a few doctors and a bag of bones." These
efforts led to the transformation of medical training in the United
States and the role of medical personnel in the better medical
schools. The health researchers found that economic underdevelop-
ment was a prime cause of sickness; thus they concentrated their
attention on regions such as the southern states.

The work the foundations began in health was eventually taken
over by governments. The National Science Foundation, the National Institute of Health, and other public bodies picked up where
the foundations left off. They were able to devote far more resources
to the task than were private foundations and to mobilize a wider
range of scientific manpower. The intervention of governmental
agencies on so massive a scale was confirmation of the principle on
which foundation-programming was based. It proved that foundations could use "risk capital" for demonstration projects and experimentation. When these efforts showed what could be done, government was able to move in and build on solid structures.

The feeding of mankind has come to be another important focal
point for foundations. The successes of international scientists working together to improve the world's health helped pave the way for
cooperative agricultural programs. One of the first fully organized

coherent international projects, as we have seen, was the Mexican Agriculture Program of the Rockefeller Foundation, proposed by a politician, Henry A. Wallace, and authorized by a humanist, Raymond Fosdick. What followed the Mexican success was the creation of the country programs discussed above (see pp. 85–86).

Foundations have also led the way in new assistance areas such as rural development, basic education, environmental studies, and the training of government planners. In some of these fields, it is true that public programs have preceded private efforts. The foundations' participation has nonetheless been of utmost importance, and though it would be premature to claim results such as those in other fields, the continued use of well-tested foundation practice cannot help but have significance for the future.

4. FOUNDATION PROGRAMMING AND FUNCTIONALIST CRITERIA   It is now possible to hold up to foundation efforts certain well-recognized functionalist criteria.

The nonpolitical criterion. Whereas foundations have conducted programs in the developing world which have, for the most part, been nonpolitical, they have also displayed a variety of patterns in their work. Although the aim has been to remain apart from local political forces, they are never wholly free. If they had insisted on total independence of government, they would have sacrificed considerably the influence they have exerted. It must also be remembered that the sharp distinction often drawn between the public and private sectors in the West, is absent or less clear in the developing world. Leaving this aside, professionals and technicians from abroad more often than not work with technicians in such government ministries as health, agriculture, and education. Successful assistance programs, moreover, normally require matching contributions by the host governments. Foreign technicians who succeed must make it their business to know and work with key officials in the host government. The founding director of the Mexican Agriculture Program of the Rockefeller Foundation, Dr. J. George Harrar, has stated that he made it his first responsibility and concern to study the personal ambitions and cultural and political viewpoints of the incumbent Mexican minister of agriculture.

All this notwithstanding, the success of cooperative educational programs has depended upon their having both the appearance and reality of being nonpolitical. Cooperation has been achieved when educators speak to educators. In most educational assistance programs abroad, official contacts with local or national politicians has been best left to the "resident representative" of the foreign group. Outsiders or American-based representatives visiting these programs have generally preferred to concentrate their visits on meetings with local educators rather than the political representatives of their own or the host country. I made it a practice in advance of any visit to contact the educators or scientists with whom I sought discussions and frequently they, rather than embassy personnel, met me at the airport and scheduled my educational appointments. In their minds, I was a nonpolitical officer of an international foundation not tarnished by strong nationalistic or colonial ambitions or caught up in my nation's struggle for power.

The nongovernmental criterion. Private assistance agencies working abroad have taken pains, however, to assure that they do not act in contravention of the policies of their own government. Cultural-exchange programs with the Soviet Union and several eastern European countries were not initiated until the public policies of the government of the United States made them acceptable. Representatives of private agencies working abroad have as a rule been somewhat reserved about establishing formal contacts with their own embassy. The courting process has often gone the other way. Some who make a creed of the separation of private American and official governmental efforts will have nothing to do with United States representatives abroad. They argue that the price in their relations with host educators or scientists—that is, of appearing to be on governmental leading strings—is too great.

The other side of this coin raises the question of keeping governmental representatives informed. It is said that the progress of the Mexican Agriculture Program would have been accelerated if governmental agencies like the International Cooperation Agency (ICA) had joined with the Rockefeller Foundation earlier to give the program a push. Instead ICA and the Rockefeller Foundation representatives kept their distance. The closest they came to communicating was when the ICA representative in Mexico asked Dr. Harrar to fill out a fifty-page application—which he promptly consigned to the wastebasket. As the priorities of private and public agencies have come to correspond with one another more and more, the distance between their representatives in the field has diminished. At home, foundation executives have become more inclined to play the political game, some having acknowledged political aspirations. Despite such stratagems, congressional investigations and the Tax Reform Act of 1969 have increased controls on foundations and held them to their nongovernmental role. Thus with respect to this criterion, the picture is a mixed one.

The social-economic criterion. Here the line between foundations and functionalism is clear. Foundations that work in the nongovernmental sector are by definition likely to be concerned with social problems such as health and education. At the same time, most of these problems have a political dimension. Beyond this, foundations have created institutes for the study of public policy and of war and peace, problems that cannot be restricted to the social sphere.

Urgent problems. From their creation, the foundations have made it clear that their focus would be on urgent problems. It was on this basis that health was chosen as the first foundation interest. The urgency of a problem has not led foundations to believe that their sole mission was to respond to crises, or merely to put out fires. Instead their accent has been on ferreting out the root causes of problems. Leaders have talked about and initiated efforts in the basic sciences, culture, the humanities, and the arts. They have lectured their nonscience colleagues on what they have called the usefulness of useless science. They have helped usher in new sciences such as biophysics and biochemistry. Their motto has been, "If you give a man a fish, he'll eat for a day; if you teach a man to fish, he'll eat for a lifetime." They have put great stress on leadership training and faculty development, rather than on the attacking of every problem directly.

Problem-centered approaches. The work of the foundations started not with a theory but a problem. It was not health in general but certain specific diseases that set in motion the first programs in health. It was not the desire to feed everyone everywhere but to help individual countries turn around their deficits in certain basic food crops that spurred the Rockefeller Foundation to inaugurate its country programs in agriculture; it was not the desire for worldwide education but the hope that a few pace-setting universities could train the doctors and agronomists, physicists and economists, engineers and managers needed in a given region. Foundation leaders from their earliest history learned one essential lesson. In philanthropy as in baseball, one scores runs only by bunching hits. Foundations can't do everything; if they are to contribute, it must be in certain well-defined areas and according to methods that are known to have worked. These areas and methods fall generally within the broad domain of functional actions.

The cooperation of professionals. The importance of professionals working together is evident throughout foundation history. Functional cooperation is not a matter for dilettantes; when programs have had a lasting impact, it has been because men of great experience and knowledge brought their talents to bear on an urgent problem. The larger foundations have drawn their staffs from professionals in the fields to which paramount attention was being given. Thus Rockefeller, until recently, has been a foundation of medical doctors, agriculturalists, and social scientists. Ford has been one of lawyers and former governmental officials. Carnegie, with a broad spectrum of concern in education and related areas, has been a foundation of generalists. Among newer philanthropies, Johnson has been one of doctors, Edna McConnell Clark of lawyers and psychologists, and Lilly of university, government, and business leaders. The smaller foundations have sometimes been no more than a banker or lawyer at the other end of a phone or, occasionally, a donor who answers his own phone. The need for professionals who work together is obviously greatest in the field. Where foundations produce results in one of the action fields, it is generally attributable to the clusters of professionals who make up an operating field staff. Having observed the value of such groups in the private sector, John Gardner, formerly president of the Carnegie Corporation and the secretary of health, education, and welfare in the Johnson administration, called on the government to set up a similar career service for educational assistance in other countries. When governmental and foundation programs fail, it is often because such personnel have not been recruited on a full-time basis, as in the ill-fated environmental program of the Rockefeller Foundation in the Hudson Basin from 1973 to 1975. When programs fail, it is frequently because new and inexperienced leaders ignore the importance of professional cooperation.

The building of habits and attitudes of cooperation. In addition to professional cooperation, there is also a cultural dimension to working abroad. Living side by side with nationals of other countries for a substantial time period can engender empathy and respect that transcend professional relations. There are few experiences as likely to change attitudes. Learning another language, sensing what is unique in other societies, and coming to understand the native lore—all these are means of throwing new light on prevailing similarities and differences among cultures. A Mexican legend warned that corn should be planted only in a certain phase of the moon. The Rockefeller team disputed this lore, only to find that at every other phase of the moon, ants destroyed the seed corn. Cooperation is assured between people of different cultures only when they agree to seek mutual understanding and build new habits and attitudes toward one another based on both rational and traditional perceptions.

Broad networks of functional cooperation. Functionalism assumes that regional or international cooperation in one field helps pave the way for cooperation in another. This seems to be confirmed in the experience of private foundations. Once an outside agency has been successful in giving help abroad, it in effect establishes an identity and a presence. Trust and respect carry over from one set of functional relations to another. Those who come later are the inheritors of a legacy of respect which they themselves have not earned. When the Rockefeller Foundation returned to Thailand in the early 1960s, its way was made easier because a Rockefeller group had helped put Thailand in touch with modern medical practices and had built a teaching hospital in the 1930s. Nothing serves international cooperation better than to be known as a member of a respected international body with named leaders and a tradition of continuity and responsibility. In India during the 1950s and 1960s, it was said that American ambassadors come and go but the country leaders of Ford and Rockefeller remain. These two leaders, Douglas Ensminger and Ralph Cummings, were symbols to the Indians of the best in American life. They had demonstrated their competence and had proven that they and their colleagues had something to offer. They were also good listeners and generally knew what the Indians wanted. Because these men and their professional colleagues were part of the culture, employed local personnel, and administered functional programs in health, education, and agriculture, they were looked upon as trusted friends. They did not speak for fly-by-night agencies, but for organizations with long-term commitments to India. Their contribution was in a broad network of functional relations that they and their hosts had established and maintained.

Transnationalism. Only a few of the largest foundations have operating programs that span national boundaries. These include Ford, Rockefeller, Carnegie (though restricted to members of the old British Commonwealth), Kellogg, and perhaps one or two others. A few more have given support to international studies. This group includes the Danforth Foundation, Lilly, Rockefeller Brothers Fund, Bydale Foundation, Compton Foundation, and Edna McConnell Clark. The fact that primary and fundamental problems know no boundaries has tended to lead to a transnational outlook. However, it is a mark of the still extant provincialism that so few foundations have selected such problems as their focus and followed where those problems led.

Sovereignty. As we have seen, functionalism anticipates that if national sovereignty is ever to be overcome, it will be by erosion, not constitutional change. There are few present signs of sovereignty being limited by political means. The foundations try to avoid being a threat to national governments. Professionals and technicians have not shown much interest in discussions of sovereignty, and it is important to remember that relations between governments and education or governments and science in most of the developing countries are far closer than in the West. This means that functional advances are more likely to augment national prestige and power than to take any of it away.

Spillover effects. This functionalist concept as related to foundations is hard to measure. It is apparent that national governments almost imperceptibly take a broader view as a result of functionalism. However, they remain sovereign states. Political leaders change; and even where the heads of functional programs have had some influence and contact, they lose it with the turnover. Still it is true that participants in functional programs exercise some degree of influence over governmental officials. Successive Mexican governments turn for advice on agriculture to George Harrar, Norman Borlaug, and Edwin Wellhausen of the original Rockefeller team. Their nationality as Americans hardly limits the role they play. In another context, cooperation has developed between some of the first-generation agricultural programs and second-generation ones. Mexico has given funds and agricultural materials and tools to certain Central American states, thus returning the debt they feel to the Rockefeller Foundation which first helped them. The influence of the functionalists on political leaders has occurred through the formers' introducing an international and even a global outlook into governmental circles. In another way, spillover has taken place. Country agricultural programs have evolved into international agricultural institutes, and ministers who administered the one have been elected to the boards of trustees of the other. Some functional specialists who begin in one country go on to staff such specialized agencies as the World Health Organization (WHO) and FAO.

What has occurred is what might be called a partial spillover, as what is accomplished in one functional area does carry over into another. Whether it persists and how lasting its influence will be depends on personal factors that cannot be measured in advance. Yet functional specialists as such do have influence on nationally oriented leaders, and to this extent what is done in a social or economic field influences the political arena.

Foundations, therefore, help to illustrate in their work both the relevance and the limitations of functionalism. They measure up to most of the functionalists' criteria, but not every result forecast by functionalism shows signs of being attained. Thus functionalism remains an insightful approach to international problems, but not one that is wholly satisfactory. In this it shares the common plight of every other important theory of international relations.

Conclusions

Because David Mitrany wrestled with one of the urgent problems in international relations—that of laying the foundations for international community through cooperation on specific problems—his influence has been considerable. The host of present-day social scientists who continue his work includes Paul Taylor and A. J. R. Groom from Great Britain and Ernst Haas and I. L. Claude from the United States.

It is tempting to see in functionalism a panacea for the problems of persistent nationalism, particularly given the failures of other approaches to international order such as world law and world government. Mitrany had no illusions regarding such a panacea, but he did hold that functional cooperation on a limited scale on defined social problems might build common interests and changed attitudes. It was an approach, not a theory, he maintained. It held out the promise of long-range advancement, not instant solutions to international problems rooted in national loyalties.

Our evidence from a review of three concrete efforts at international cooperation in higher education, international agriculture, and the work of the larger private foundations with international programs lends some credence to the functional approach. Such efforts would appear to suggest that functional endeavors are able to proceed along lines that more direct and explicit political programs by nation-states would find impossible. At the same time, these efforts hardly prove that technical cooperation can lead to political cooperation with attendant erosion of national sovereignty. The problem may differ from efforts in the developed world involving "regulatory functionalism" and the cooperation of industrial states toward some form of political or more often economic integration and "developmental functionalism" of the kind exemplified in the three case studies discussed above. In the latter case, the spillover effect would seem to be the opposite of that envisaged by Mitrany. Success leads to the politicization of functionalism.

Nonetheless, functionalism deserves study in the era of world interdependence. And its thesis that social and economic cooperation on specific problems can be more readily achieved than new federal systems can be established has merit that cannot be dismissed.

IV

The Problems
of Power,
Nationalism, and
the Future

The crisis in values and the search for a relevant framework of
thought take on concreteness only when we approach specific problems. It is one thing to talk abstractly about values and the competition among them; it is another thing to experience their impact in
personal life. The solemnity of having to choose among those to
whom one has made commitments, thereby neglecting another, cannot be explained away in the simplistic language of game theory. It
may be clever gamesmanship to speak of "coming out even" in
moral choices by giving a little here and adding something there,
thus achieving a zero sum game; but this obscures the fact that man
is a moral as well as a social animal. He feels deep anguish in choices
he must make; and whereas social psychology and present-day
therapy would ostensibly rid him of all guilt, he remains uneasy
with himself and his moral predicament, whatever the analytical or
mathematical scheme put forth. It may be fashionable and even for
the most part healthful to release human beings from a guilt-ridden
state; but if social scientists and mental-health personnel were to
succeed in eliminating the tension men feel between what they are
and what they would like to be, then our lives might lose much of
their creative and dynamic thrust.

It is also commonplace in some quarters to speak of theories as
being remote from life. Americans are a practical people, impatient
with high-sounding and far-flung generalizations. Once more, how-

ever, if life is to have any meaning, we need to find ways of breaking through the endless repetition of seemingly unconnected events that make up most of it. If men of thought stand aside, ideologues will step into the breach. From earliest childhood most of us are exposed to a perfectly astounding number of "explanations" that seek to account for the world around us. Some are based on scapegoating; others are essentially "devil theories," and the vast majority rest on misconceptions and misinformation. It is vital, therefore, that responsible thinkers help us to understand the world. The need is especially urgent because policy-makers flounder not so much in their mastery of the facts but in the building of coherent frameworks that give meaning to the facts they interpret—witness Vietnam, for example.

Yet values and theories are of little use if they remain on the bookshelf. Their utility and truth must be tested in the social arena. Social science in this respect is not the same as the biological or natural sciences. The physical scientist at work in his laboratory is largely free to pursue his research wherever the last experiment takes him, without being judged by the immediate use to which his work can be put. Society is and will remain the primary laboratory for the social scientist.

Man's problems are too overwhelming, his perplexities too unsettling, and the burden of his choices too oppressive for him not to seek meaning where he can find it. His uncertainty and concern are especially great in three areas: his view of the future, of America's role in the twenty-first century, and of the relationship between American social and educational values and those of the so-called Third World. Reflections on all three areas are influenced by value judgments. Understanding depends on the existence of one or more coherent intellectual frameworks. Values and theories are put to work when we consider the three areas. Taken together they constitute a proving ground for what has been said up to now in the discussion of the problem of values, of ethics in war and peace, and of functionalism and world order.

The Last Quarter-Century:
Change as Challenge—
or Catastrophe

Because most of us are "little conservatives" or "little liberals," we are baffled, divided, and troubled by change. Most of our judgments about change reflect in some measure our varying temperaments and styles. Either we function best with things as they are in familiar surroundings when stimuli and responses are predictable and routine, or we demand bold new challenges and large opportunities if life is to be worth living. It is the beginning of wisdom to recognize that in our response to change, we are not the same and we do not help one another by blind insistence that we are. There is no such thing as one objective response to change, for each of us responds from the ground on which we stand. In the late 1960s a whole generation, not given to particularly modest goal formulations, confronted the rest of society. This generation said that it was not, and did not intend to be, merely its father's children. Given the excesses and self-indulgence of some phases of the youth movement, we are tempted to view their rebellion as a rather unhealthy aberration, not in keeping with the untroubled advance of civilization. Our response might be more constructive if, for this somewhat painful era, we could sift out the wheat from the chaff and use it to learn an important lesson. Buffeted by winds of change and coping in our varied ways with the contradictions and inconsistencies of the culture, we are each pilgrims striving to hold to an uncertain and essentially uncharted course. As Lincoln put it, we would know better what to do if we knew whither we were tending, but for today this seems largely denied and beyond us.

It is of course a truism that change for all men everywhere is the first law of the universe. For those of us whose parents and grandparents were immigrants, personal history refutes the proposition that the past was a succession of known, predictable, and settled events. Those ancestors made their way across a continent as strange in its languages, customs, and people as in its vast expanse and

107

unexplored frontiers. Some triumphed over suffering and adversity
and are celebrated as "giants in the earth"; others, including those
who had known success in other lands, fought valiantly to cope with
changes only to succumb to forces beyond their control. They went
to their graves with unfulfilled hopes and the dream of a promised
land which, in their lives, had proved too harsh and demanding to
realize. They left to others who came after them the rewards of
achieving "life, liberty, and the pursuit of happiness"; they were
victims of a new world for which they were unsuited, in which they
were disappointed, unlucky, ill-fated.

Yet whether for those who found success and a new life or those
who failed while only dimly aware of America's possibilities, existence was grounded on certain fixed points and givens. Most of them
had faith that hard work would bring both material and spiritual
rewards. They prayed to the same God, read the same historical
texts, held to the same attitudes toward church, state, and society;
they struggled to preserve family loyalties and community structures. Their doubts centered more on the capriciousness of nature
than on the unpredictability of human nature. They knew enough to
respect the violence and destructiveness of weather, but not enough
to prevent their immobilization before man's uncontrolled passions
and the fury of human storms unleashed in civilized mass societies.
They knew the pain if not all the causes of individual breakdowns;
but they did not know the cataclysmic effect of the breakdowns of
societies in holocausts, total wars, thermonuclear peril, and worldwide economic disruptions. They had national pride, but not the
fanatical national self-righteousness that justified the wholesale
slaughter of millions of German Jews or Russian kulaks to further a
single national cause. They did wrong, spilled blood, and took the
lives of native peoples who blocked their march across the continent; but their cruelty was less rationally organized and totally sanc-
tified than Nazism or the Leninist-Stalinist version of communism
in which religion, historical inevitability, and nationalism were
inextricably joined. "If we had done for ourselves what we did
for the state what scoundrels we would have been," wrote Italian
nationalist Count Camillo Benso Cavour. For earlier American gen

erations, there were countervailing powers that kept imperial conquest and national ambition in check. More importantly, men's lives were anchored in a set of unchanging beliefs and convictions. Some of us have known the majesty of such a faith in our parents and grandparents. At my mother's death in 1976, I wrote the following lines:

> Her joy was in service to others—service given with such selflessness and grace that no one could say she made them dependent—the curse of so much self-conscious giving....
>
> She praised God not by words but through the example of her life.... She taught that anything worth doing was worth doing well—from perfecting a concerto to counselling a child.... By the power of gentleness and kindness, she drew out some of the pain from raw open wounds.... Whatever the problem, she listened and understood and, for me at least, the warmth of her living room took the place of the minister's study or the psychiatrist's couch.
>
> Yet all her gentler virtues could never explain her 95 years. She was driven by an inner fire. Her determination had roots in deep-seated spiritual resources and her tireless heart sustained a frail body until the very end.... She remained busy even in her final reveries, concerned for others when confused, aware of human pathos when perplexed about her own.
>
> What crowned all her hard work, patience and sympathy, trust and determination and made her loneliness tolerable was her love of God, family and friends, life and music.
>
> Love led to service to others, to the search for worthy ends, to doing for herself by doing for others.[1]

There were others who saw in her life qualities that set her apart and made her life a timeless example. A very wise physician who called on her two and three times each day during her final illness observed: "They don't make them like that any more." He might have added that the structure of faith and values that nurtured her and provided the fixed points in her life had also died for most of the culture decades before her passing. The serenity she felt in life and which even in facing death kept aflame the will to live is not present for most of us today. And this lack, as much as the kaleidescopes of change, is the major source of our troubles. Neither cynicism about values nor easy moral rhetoric can remove the predicament. It is a predicament which can lead either to a sense of catastrophe or to a heightened awareness of challenges that test to the limit man's innermost resources. Quiet reflection and intellectual honesty prompt recognition that most of us, at one time or another, experience alternately quiet desperation or renewed resolve in facing the future. It will not do for educators either to expound on opportunity and ignore the crisis or to talk only of the crisis. It is vital that we view the problem of change through the eyes of those who anticipate catastrophe no less than through those that are awakened to unprecedented challenges.

1. CATASTROPHE The most poignant moment of the 1976 Republican national convention was a late evening televised conversation from Kansas City between Vice-President Nelson Rockefeller and Senator Barry Goldwater. Bitter political foes through the 1950s and 1960s, the two found themselves embracing each other in 1976, in substantial accord on most major issues. Probing for an explanation for their new-found unity, Walter Cronkite asked Mr. Rockefeller to explain the reasons. The former governor of New York, whose administration had brought the powers of government forcefully to bear on the economy, education, public works, and the building of a vast transportation network for the state, acknowledged rather plaintively that most if not all of these programs had failed. It was his experience, he confessed, that government lacked the know-how and the skills, the resources and the manpower, and the will to solve or even to mitigate the intractable problems of the day. What flashed through the mind of at least one viewer was another political convention in Chicago eight years earlier, when long lines of youthful protesters chanted that the system was not working and at best should be given only one more chance. From both the left and the right we hear that the government is not working—and we hear this too often for these melancholy words not to give us pause.

If partisan political declarations were the only indicators of crisis and catastrophe, we might have less cause for alarm, but the root causes run deeper. They extend from the first signs that the nation's civilization may be going the way of past civilizations, about which historians from Edward Gibbon to Arnold J. Toynbee have written— to the breakup and decline of long-established social and political institutions: the nation-state, the church, the family, to mention but three. When Secretary of State Kissinger, in a moment of political indiscretion, noted that America's position as the one preeminent world power might be passing, he unleashed a small army— and navy!—of critics. Yet Kissinger may have been more prophetic than those who denounced him.

What is unique about the present crisis, whether seen as a whole or as it touches specific institutions, is that old values and patterns appear to be losing their hold, though new ones are not taking their place. The nation-state for all practical purposes is inadequate if not obsolete in an interdependent world, but neither world government (of which one hears less and less) nor strong regional political systems are having much success. The family is in decline or is being reshaped to a point that scarcely if at all resembles its basic and integral character. As one young man observed, the trouble with the alternatives is the almost total absence of rules and dependable mutual responsibilities. Religion and tradition across a broad spectrum ranging from art to reverence for life have been brought into question or recast in postmodern terms in which anything goes. Yet art without standards is no better than life without values, not because worthy goals are ever fully realized (this was the fallacy of the mass indictments leveled by middle-class young people against their parents in the late 1960s) but because human potential is realized only in the tension between the ideal and the real.

According to an ancient Indonesian saying, it is a terrible thing to have a reasonable father. For young people the need has never been greater to test their ideas against firmly held parental ideals, not a moral and intellectual vacuum. Because we have had, in contemporary society, too much authoritarianism in the relationship between those who exercise power—whether the imperial presidency or the authoritarian father—and those whose fate is shaped by such power, we have moved toward assuming that no one need ever to be in charge. Yet instinctively, we know that a leaderless society brings

111

little happiness and peace of mind. When a president such as Harry S. Truman takes charge and makes decisions, he grows in stature as historians review and reassess his administration. Because society has lost faith that it can solve its problems, it acclaims those who rise to meet the challenge.

Yet for most Americans the moments of celebration are few and far between. Kenneth Clark tells us that the heaviest toll taken by the ghetto in American cities is the destruction of all hope for its inhabitants. The sense of impotence to effect change is, however, no monopoly of black people in urban areas. If there was political apathy in the 1976 presidential election, it stemmed in part from doubts that anyone in high office could make a difference. As one journalist writing postmortem in the Washington *Post* after the election observed: the best efforts of the last four presidents ended in disaster, disgrace, or defeat. What reason was there to expect that a successor, whatever his promises, could make a difference? Society was out of control, and it appeared that nothing could be done to bring it under control.

If we look beyond both the election and individual leaders to the more general causes of despair and apocalyptic thinking, other factors are contributory. Some may continue to elude our best thought and imagination, but others are not beyond repair. One has to do with what René DuBois calls the autonomy of science. Science by its own momentum makes policy decisions for mankind. Technology provides the means of building larger and faster airplanes, armaments ever more lethal and destructive, automobiles demanding more gasoline and larger highways and producing more and more pollution. The physicist, Herbert F. York, explains that for armaments the line separating basic research and development from procurement and production is virtually indistinguishable. Once scientists have demonstrated conclusively that the latest armaments are feasible, they will have begun the procurement process. The ability to produce new weaponry becomes tantamount to its production. It becomes increasingly difficult for the citizen decision-maker to break into the process and arrest the building of new defense systems once scientists establish their feasibility. The decision on the supersonic transport by the Congress may be the exception to what has seemed an irreversible chain of events.

Another contributing factor to the public's sense of impotence is the lack of a relevant framework for understanding the rapidly moving events that whirl around the bewildered citizen. For the future, it will not be enough to say the people should be trusted and then bury them in a blizzard of reports of seemingly unconnected and unexplained events. Political messages in election campaigns, as well as the daily barrage of rapid-fire evening news items, are delivered in 60-second capsules interspersed with 45-second commercials— leaving context and background to the citizen's ignorance, uncertainty, and prejudice. What is needed at every point are anchors for the culture; and neither politicians, newsmen, nor model-building social scientists and philosophers are filling the void. Consequently, society is bereft of moorings and grounding.

Education, which for most of mankind has been its last best hope, is itself contributing to the present malaise. In the 1960s, a leading American foundation announced that it was prepared to assist scholars who proposed to study major foreign policy problems visible on the horizon two, three, or five years hence but not currently on the agenda of the secretary of state. The announcement brought less than a handful of responses—in contrast with a flood of proposals on simulation studies, model building, and decision-making theories.

In moments of candor, we educators who feverishly pursue our interests need to admit that no area of human endeavor is more dominated by fads and fashions than ours, more controlled by old and new establishments and cliques, more swept along by currently acceptable dogmas and methodologies. We need to recognize that there is a perfectly astounding amount of intolerance in the scholarly world. I have repeatedly observed the process at work, whereby the "outs" became the "ins" and heterodox and unorthodox thinkers created their own orthodoxies. Once they had influence, those who had long been denied entrance to the corridors of power slammed the doors to others coming after them. Indeed, it is difficult to name over any significant time period more than a very few academic

113

thinkers whose influence on public policy broadly conceived has made a difference. The fragmentation of education and research leads to the isolating of one aspect of a problem—and to the pretense that understanding it means understanding the whole. The rash of investigations of human sexuality (some undoubtedly long overdue), which equate statistical evidence on the percentage rate of sexual gratification among white urban females, aged twenty-three to twenty-seven, with long and happy marriages, is only the latest example of such fragmentation or compartmentalizing of knowledge.

It is not surprising, therefore, that from no group more than the educators have lamentations been greater concerning the impending catastrophe. One publicist wrote that while scholars fiddled, the cities and bomb-packed world were burning. Although this indictment is probably too severe, those of us who live our days in the cloistered academic world need to acknowledge that, all too often, major initiatives for response to change come not from intellectuals but from the man on the street. Education, which ought to be in the vanguard, often brings up the rear. The great issues of values, of justice and peace, of equality and order are evidently too complex for academics to chew. Although there are signs that the prevailing school of value-free social science is dispirited and divided, its numbers and influence persist. Paging through the journals will quell any doubts. The scholarly world stands fragmented and divided, atomized and quantified, counting and refining in the face of life-and-death decisions that call for profound value choices.

There is deep pathos in education's tragic failure to see change as challenge, not catastrophe. The root cause of man's problem in coping with change is one for which educated thinkers have what economists call a comparative advantage. We tend to see the apocalypse in each new expression of change because we are crippled by a sense of powerlessness. The great choices that lie before us all seem to require some form of collective action. Faced by this, the solitary individual resigns himself to a feeling of impotence and inertia. Our problems are so immense, so complicated, so difficult that individuals conclude there is little or nothing they can do. Questions of justice and a just society lie beyond the reach, say, of logical positivism and linguistic analysis; for the present-day philosopher, in comparison with William James or Reinhold Niebuhr, justice loses its sense of immediacy and urgency. Once-hallowed issues of moral reasoning are pushed aside in the practical management of large hospitals, prisons, and schools, to say nothing of big government. Thus apathy and inertia take the place of compassion and a social conscience. Educators put the capstone on a moral and intellectual atmosphere that accepts the possibility of catastrophe. Reality is too large for microtheory. Yet is is precisely in the area where mind and spirit meet that classical education has traditionally made its most lasting contribution.

2. CHALLENGE Fortunately the failure of education and of society in general to meet novel and apparently insoluble problems of change is not universal. Often on the periphery of establishment groups in education and public policy, there are signs of a qualitatively different approach. Harvard's greatest legal scholar, Paul Freund, calls for a return to the ancient tradition of moral reasoning. John Rawls, professor of philosophy at Harvard, through his treatise on justice has stirred discussion and controversy reminiscent of the debates that went on in the Harvard of William James, William Ernest Hocking, and Josiah Royce. The literature of the past several decades in international relations has thrown the spotlight on the conflicting imperatives of national interest and world order. The Institute of Society, Ethics, and the Life Sciences at the Hastings Center deals in the October, 1976 issue of its *Report* with such topics as "The Right to Die in California," "Sterilizing the Poor and the Incompetent," and "The Legal Right to Health Care." New journals on philosophy and public policy are springing up, and a seven-university consortium fellowship program chooses world order and world politics as its organizing theme. President Carter conducted a winning campaign unashamedly centering on "love and justice," and the electorate apparently found a note of credibility in the claim that too few people have acquired too much power within the geographical confines of one city.

The road ahead toward the reconstructuring of values is long and tortuous, and there is as much reason to fear as to rejoice over the first faint signs of response. It is one thing to write or talk of justice and another to point the way to implementing it. The French philosopher Paul Ricouer has helped to crystalize our thinking by suggesting that the day of the lonely individual Good Samaritan has passed, and that we are today witnessing the effort to filter such justice and compassion as we know through vast sprawling networks of public and private bureaucracy. For health care, old-age retirement, and unemployment, such bureaucracies constitute the machinery by which society seeks to give each man his due. Our ethicists implore us to understand that the ethical must be spelled out in countless settings, adapted and readapted for specific situations. And all this occurs within the exigencies of time and change. Trying to do what is right involves making choices under circumstances of flux. The policy-maker must act, as does the hunter following a bird in flight. If his aim is wrong or he fails to lead his prey, he gets only tail feathers for his trouble.

Moreover, today's changes are legion and many-sided, with ramifications in all directions. Government must help us meet our more pressing problems, some of which can be dealt with only for society as a whole. But government has had its chance, especially since the days of Franklin D. Roosevelt. And if we have learned nothing else from nearly five decades of experience with big government, it is that no sector—whether public or private—has a monopoly on wisdom and justice. Warning signs have gone up, telling us that a healthy economy atrophies when too large a segment of non-wage earners draws too heavy a percentage of income from the taxes of an ever-smaller segment of the producers of goods and services. Voluntarism, which writers from Alexis de Tocqueville to David Riesman have singled out as unique to the American system, is threatened when powerless men resign themselves to letting George do it, particularly when George is in far-off Washington. Therefore, the future promises a host of ever-shifting and experimental patterns of governmental relations, some highly centralized but others marked by the type of decentralized efforts that have been called for by John Gardner, former secretary of health, education, and welfare and founder of Common Cause. In every field of public endeavor, including diplomacy, innovations are likely. We have tried public diplomacy, bilateral and multilateral negotiations, quiet diplomacy, and shuttle diplomacy; and, depending on the interests at stake, each has its merits and its disadvantages. If we are able to keep personal vanity and pride of authorship in check, we may yet discover the most appropriate diplomatic machinery for meeting new challenges and preventing worldwide self-destruction.

It is obvious that another of the severest challenges in the years ahead will come in the workings of the economy. If one issue predominated in the 1976 elections, it was the economy, specifically inflation and unemployment. No field of social sciences takes as much pride as economics in the rigor of its methods and the precision of its forecasting, yet none was more dramatically brought up short by dominant economic trends. Nor were the practitioners of applied economics in banks and business more prescient than the scholars. It is *infra dig* among economic scientists to urge that some of the concerns of what once was called political economy deserve reexamination. Econometrics and microtheory have evolved tools of analysis far more sophisticated than policy-oriented studies of an earlier day. With the manifold forms of interaction between government and the economy, however, the focus of economics must, in part at least, be addressed once more to the politics of the economy. At the same time, the oil crisis has helped us to see that a national approach to economics is not enough. Large corporations that make use of political consultants are conscious of the need, and it is high time our best economists looked beyond national boundaries if they are to make their science operationally relevant. Some younger economists are manifesting an interest in the economics of education, of cities, and of oil; and while the terminology may offend the more orthodox, the need is too pressing to justify the arguments of the purists.

Change expresses itself also in demands that more attention be given to the quality of life. In every one of the less-developed countries, national leaders with whom I have worked have explained that increasing the Gross National Product, though a worthy national goal, was not sufficient. They have been frank to say that they did

117

not wish to run the cycle of industrialization-commercialization-pollution-urban blight that the developed countries have followed, though trends in the richer developing countries point that way. Developing-country leaders are in search of innovative educational structures more appropriate to their needs. They are coming forward with rural-development strategies that aim at increasing the use of intermediate technologies, lifelong learning, technical-vocational training, and assistance to indigenous entrepreneurs. The twin goals of the so-called poorer nation are to gear education more directly to community problems, thus closing the gap between work and study, and to define national goals more concretely in order to generate support among the people. The forms and structures through which the poorer countries are working hardly correspond to those of the richer countries.

The best way to earn stripes as an "ugly American" is to judge the social and political life of one's hosts during the first twenty-four or forty-eight hours of a visit. There is much Americans can learn from these nations (for example, regarding education for development), and a possible meeting ground is a common heightened awareness that the quality of life deserves greater stress. Within the United States, changing work patterns and life styles demand reconsideration. The four-day work week is becoming increasingly common, and early retirement for various occupations occurs as often in one's fifties as in the sixties. The mechanization of certain kinds of work forces lively and energetic people to look for satisfaction outside their places of major employment. In my youth, leisure time for most was in short supply. Now almost every locality has its adult-education programs, its recreational offerings, and numerous community programs of varying importance. Community colleges, which Harold Howe II, formerly commissioner of education, calls the single great twentieth century educational innovation, are filling an urgent need for adults returning to complete their education. Repertory theaters have sprung up in many communities, and local symphonies and dance groups provide a rich cultural life.

In viewing the developed and less-developed countries, what I find most striking is the crucial role that cultural development has

come to play in both. In less-developed countries, cultural development serves as the route to national integration. Most of the new
nations lack the main requisites of nationalism. They are at best
loosely organized collections of tribes, brought together by the accident of colonial settlements. For such peoples, a sense of culture
plays a paramount role in national unification; without it they are
unlikely to know what it means to be a Nigerian or a Tanzanian.

In the developed countries, culture faces a different challenge.
Here the identity crisis is less national and more individual. With
more people spending more time away from their jobs, and with
work itself, as the late Hannah Arendt wrote, frequently taking on
attributes of drudgery rather than dignity, the individual must find
meaning and purpose for life outside his job. He must choose between
cultural or civic activities capable of producing continued personal
growth and the endless repetition of late childhood adventures
guaranteeing a state of permanent adolescence.

A related social problem, which may prove the greatest challenge, should be mentioned here. America leads the world in its
scandalous treatment of the aging. Driven from their homes, they
languish in second-class nursing centers which are at best an invitation to perpetual loneliness. It is scant consolation that the other
developed countries have fallen into similarly disgraceful patterns.
Until not long ago Japan had been a country in which 75 percent of
the aged lived with and were revered by their families. The Japanese
now house most of their older people in public establishments. Recently a dying Japanese woman who had been a long-time resident
in such a paradise left all her earthly belongings to her television set,
the only object with which, according to her will, she had had any
communication in the last fifteen years of her life.

This leads to the last item on the agenda, our communications
network. No one can fault America for its technological achievements. Modern television is the most powerful instrument known to
man for the instantaneous communication of news of the nation's
business. It is capable of bringing art and education into the living
room of the poorest family. Potentially it is the world's greatest
educator and human equalizer. Yet for many of our citizens it has

119

become an opiate, a substitute for responsible participation. We are drenched in soap operas, schooled in the latest forms of violence, and deprived of the deepest mysteries of the human drama. Television offers the public the lowest common denominator of American life. It claims to provide what the people want. It simplifies and corrupts the nation's most basic dialogues, including the political and international.

This is plain talk, and not pleasant. Any balanced treatment must hasten to give praise and credit for those occasional national services that TV has rendered, such as its coverage of Watergate, the walk on the moon, and the Vietnam War, to say nothing of good cultural programs. The challenge posed, however, is that we are capable of doing so much better, not only with communications but with the care of the aged, cultural development, the quality of life, the workings of the economy, and the ordering of political life. It is defeatist to think and act as if improvements lay beyond human imagination and will. We need a reordering of priorities and a restructuring of institutions. Profits and power may be essential in society, but so is a renewed sense of service. Rights are a part of the heritage, but so are responsibilities. If self-esteem requires that we think more about the self, then a good society means we ought not to neglect the common good. In rejecting the traditional forms and institutions of Western values, we have abandoned what is far more important: their substance.

Is there a way to renew the essence of the heritage? I suggest that the answer lies in a return to moral reasoning. Moral reasoning is the discipline of weighing and considering competing and sometimes conflicting rights and wrongs. Moral choice involves the ordering of rights that compete with other rights and the limitations one places on the others. The rights of the majority can never justify extinguishing all rights for the minority. If Americans would restore this type of thinking in all the manifold areas in which we must respond to change, we might proceed within a coherent framework of thought. We might then see change as a challenge, not a castastrophe.

3. A CONCLUDING NOTE   No one can forecast with assurance the directions history will take in the next quarter century. As British

historian H. L. A. Fisher argued in a brilliant essay, no task is more uncertain and bewildering: "We know more about the world in which we live and are in a better position to gauge the forces which move it. Our statistics are more complete, our knowledge of the past is fuller." But, Fisher warned, although we have gained in precision, "the factors to be assessed have increased in number and complexity. In place of the isolated rivalries of the past, we are now faced with struggles in which the whole habitable globe is either directly or indirectly involved. The problems have become so vast, their solution depends on a forecast of so many imponderables and concurrent factors, upon so vast a complexus of doubtful contingencies, that statesmanship ... has become three parts guesswork." [2]

With all the refinements of methods and technology, we still depend on social imagination, political judgment, and human wisdom. Fisher points out in a review of political prophets the unique prescience of a small group of political thinkers, including Burke, Polybius, de Tocqueville, and Sir John Seeley. He offers a longer list of those whose historical judgments were far from the mark. If we consider present-day thinkers and rank them, as Fisher did his thinkers, we note that Lippmann warned of the risks of a land war in Asia, Niebuhr prophesied that the United States would not be accepted or admired everywhere in the Third World in part because of our power and wealth, and Morgenthau proclaimed that successful foreign policy had to reflect the national interest, not a moral crusade. It remains true, even in the age of the computer, that all human intelligence as it reaches out to comprehend the future is not equal. In Fisher's words "the higher gifts of divination ... depend upon an insight into the fundamental moral forces of the world." [3]

In this sense William Wordsworth was superior to statesmen like William Pitt or Napoleon. Wordsworth foresaw in the rise of Spain an instrument for thwarting French imperialism, the need to curb the abuses of child labor, and other evils of industrialism; he anticipated national compulsory education and the corruption of the popular press. The goal in these complex human areas is, as the British say, to get it right, and rightness here includes both justice and clarity.

I would advocate a call for greater openness and sympathy for the

121

thought and writings of the exceptional few whose minds bring us closer to the truth, thinkers who are more than compilers, conceptualizers, or classifiers. You will ask, "How does one recognize them?" And I would reply, "By their words, and the quality more than the quantity of their words." But to know them, one must also know oneself—the gravity of one's commitments, concerns, and questions—and one's resolve to seek the truth. I challenge anyone with deep and abiding concerns and questions on democracy to read de Tocqueville without sensing that here is such a mind. I ask anyone with commitments to true progress to read Carl Becker without a similar enlightenment. And who among us can read Hannah Arendt without gaining a new understanding of totalitarianism? We will not find the works of such writers and prophets on the list of best sellers or reported prominently in *Publisher's Weekly*. It is unlikely that large publishers will have pulled out all the stops of their public relations machinery for them, at least not while they are alive. (I am told that most of Carl Becker's books sold an average of eight hundred to a thousand copies each.) I recently completed a volume called *Interpreters and Critics of the Cold War*—a review of the four or five most penetrating thinkers whose interpretations help us comprehend the Cold War better than do those of either the official or the revisionist historians. Several publishers responded that since two of my interpreters were dead and the others were not conducting empirical research projects, their work had been superseded. Fortunately, one publisher had a different view.

Publishers notwithstanding, when it comes to interpreting the future or comprehending the past, our only recourse is to the exceptional few. Where we see catastrophe or contradictions, they may bring to light some neglected source of explanation. If change is considered a challenging opportunity, these few may help plot the way to meet it and respond. It remains true that behind every major shift in policy direction, there is, as Lord Keynes so graphically put it, some oftentimes obscure academic scribbler. Behind understanding, there is often a book. The great challenge is to seek out the interpreters and critics who provide this resource. Unless we find them and ponder their thought, insights, and conclusions, we will probably remain suspended between dreams and despair, challenge and catastrophe, resolve and resignation when faced with a dangerous, uncertain, and awesome future. It will not do to condemn the system and fall into a deep and self-righteous sleep. If we are to do more than blame others and condemn our fate, however, we shall need all the accumulated resources of mankind, ancient and modern.

America and the World: Looking into the Third Century

Looking into our nation's third century so obviously exceeds a man's reach that the first reaction is to find a way to restate the challenge. A former secretary of state, when asked how he handled congressional hearings, replied that when he was asked a question he could not answer, he answered another one. It may be possible to see a few years ahead, but who can claim a quarter-century of forward vision? That remarkable group of men who made up the first policy planning staff in the Department of State under Secretary of State George C. Marshall discovered that looking ahead beyond the span of three to five years was a practical impossibility. They also learned that if the planner was to influence foreign policy he needed to become an operator; this restricted attention to more immediate problems and narrowed the span of relevant planning to a year or two, if that.

Yet scholars and informed observers continue to hear the call for responsible forecasting, and the more brash among us appear unable to resist. At one level it is possible to defend attempts to foresee what lies ahead. President Kingman Brewster of Yale distinguishes among four types of knowledge and higher learning. The first type is information-gathering, which includes the storage and retrieval of knowledge, as well as applied science which for over a decade has been on the threshold of audiovisual revolution. We have been hearing of the little black box attached to a television set, of the Socratic computer for trial and error in home learning, or of packaging Kenneth Clark's or Alistair Cooke's programs on civilization on film or cassette for the user's convenience. The second type is the acquisition of skills, a process benefiting from new techniques of audio-visual self-education, including language laboratories for the parlor, training through films in the use of computers, and hundreds of simple mathematical and mechanical operations. The third type is the testing, or trying out, of the capacity for critical judgment, whether of what Brewster calls plausible assessment or moral evaluation. It is what the historian Burkhardt called the knack of sizing up. The fourth type overlaps with judgment; it is discovery, which involves developing new insights worthy enough to deserve critical assessment. The last two efforts set to sea beyond the fixed shores of hard, indisputable information. Describing them, Brewster asserts that they "cannot be packaged or programmed ... [or] learned in a closet ... [or] learned passively. Even the most sophisticated 'Socratic computer' will not be able to provoke that free-ranging argument which holds unorthodox, genuinely original insights up to the light of scrutiny by discussion and debate. 'Thinking out loud' is indispensable to this process. The spur of rigorous discourse is itself the provocation to more adequate critical thought."[4]

Proceeding on the assumption that any ideas set down in "plausible assessment" of the future are an invitation to discourse, not a set of answers, and that for none do we have hard information, I would suggest four important areas for judgment and discovery: American leadership in the world, techniques of diplomacy, democracy and the Third World, and global human survival. No sound thinkers would claim to have a vision of likely historical developments for any of these spheres or a firm grasp of the meaning of the past quarter-century's patterns. The most anyone can do is to offer some quite tentative thoughts and impressions.

1. AMERICAN LEADERSHIP   For no other aspect of American life is there more extravagant generalization, especially before, during, and just after election time. It is not that there are no issues concerning the nature and quality of America's leadership in the world. It is rather that each of us wants that leadership to reflect our own most cherished value (normally proclaimed in the singular). And leader-

ship, we seem to say, must be widely applauded to be believed, as if there were no such thing as an action taken merely because it was right. By contrast with this all-too-prevalent view, the lessons of history teach that the most to be hoped for by strong and generous nations is a modicum of trust and respect, leaving expressions of love and gratitude to the more intimate communities of mankind. This is a lesson nations obviously have not learned when they threaten to withdraw from the world because others fail to thank and praise them.

Leadership is measured in another rather singular and myopic frame of reference. Because international society is largely anarchic and ungoverned today, a nation is judged by its ability to work its will. With force remaining the final arbiter, foreign policy demands the capacity to mobilize and apply military power. Throughout most of American history a struggle has gone on between those who deny power and those who simplify and absolutize power. America has suffered from a near fatal illness that reflects the influence on policy-makers of those two viewpoints—the one leading us in the name of American virtue and purity to hold our hand until the eleventh hour, and the other imputing absolute righteousness and justice to any use of American power.

What need concern us here is not the subject to which American historians have given much attention—the relationship of these past eras of isolationalism and of American crusades for unconditional surrender or the war to end wars or to make the world safe for democracy. This tendency to judge American leadership almost exclusively by the willingness to use force reflects a certain primitivism in national life. Since the Vietnam War, one segment of the nation's political and scholarly elite tells us that the nation will never again use force to intervene in international conflicts, and spokesmen for another school of thought declare with equal certainty that only through demonstrated capacity to use force can America arrest its precipitous decline in world leadership. If the two viewpoints were advanced with some humility and reserve, we would have less cause for alarm. The noninterventionists, however, speak with all the fervor of religious and political converts, and the champions of bold military initiatives make their case as though the opposition were composed of traitors and faithless turncoats. Both groups view their critics through glazed and blindered eyes; both listen with ears that cannot or will not hear. Not only are they ready to condemn a whole people for differing with them, but they rehearse their strengths on the slightest provocation. Each has taken hold of a portion of the reality of America's influence in the world, but mistakenly supposes it understands the whole. It is as false to maintain that the world will think well of us solely because of our noninterventionism as it is to believe we have come to the end of an era because we did not use force in Angola.

What Americans need most to relearn is that for nations as for individuals power is more than force. The lasting contribution of Reinhold Niebuhr and a handful of writers sympathetic to his views is the emphasis they have placed on the intangible as well as the tangible aspects of power. Prestige, Niebuhr wrote, is a measure of a nation's influence in the world and comprises its reputation for justice no less than the might of its arms. The quest for justice, however, is the source of America's moral predicament, for as the leaders of a triumphant Grand Alliance in World War II, we have found ourselves playing the role of the principal status-quo power in the postwar era. The depth of our predicament has been obscured by the underlying values of a liberal and humane society espousing national self-determination and proclaiming in the councils of states the end of the colonial era. Yet the decline of our influence with the new majority in the United Nations is testimony to the persistence of the predicament. To speak as though a few misguided policies or leaders were responsible, as liberals and radicals have done, or to say that because we are strong and privileged we need not continue to struggle for justice around the globe, as conservatives and reactionaries have done, is a disservice to ourselves and our heritage. One can go further and suggest in more general terms that historically bold proclamations of national or international purpose not followed by political action may actually work harm in international politics. Noble declarations such as the Atlantic Charter and the Yalta Declaration on Liberated Europe were disregarded after World

War II, thus planting seeds of doubt about America's will and intention. Serenity of purpose and moderation in words may be the better
part of wisdom, if not necessity, for a great world power. A nation
that seeks to be a world leader in the quest for justice must always be
conscious of the uncertainties and ambiguities of justice. An ancient
diplomatic saying needs recalling: what is just on this side of the
Pyrenees is not just on the other side of the Pyrenees. Defining and
applying international justice may be the most perplexing issue of
foreign policy.

American leadership, therefore, is a product of national purpose
as well as national power. It rests not on one, but on multiple factors
of tradition and policy. Political scientists who are children of the
age of specialization and the tribute society pays them have themselves reinforced the tendency to speak out exclusively for defense
policy or ideology or Third World relationships. Paradoxically, early
postwar writings on power held to a broader view than most present-
day studies that equate military strategy and power. Policy-makers
who have fought to rally support within the government for their
own vision of American leadership have difficulty transcending
that perspective. These tendencies, however understandable, should
be resisted, along with the conclusions that flow from a too-narrow
perspective on the elements of Americans' influence in the world.

2. DIPLOMACY   As we look toward the third century of our history,
the form and character of American diplomacy provides another
focal point for reflection. Much of the discussion has taken shape
around concepts of the old and new diplomacy. Traditional diplomacy through resident ambassadors and special envoys was an early
target for criticism and debate. Secret diplomacy was condemned as
a principle cause of war, and the United Nations was heralded as the
means of putting an end to the nefarious practices of European diplomacy and to the balance of power. Yet the proud boasts of President Franklin D. Roosevelt and of Secretary of State Cordell Hull that
the new international institution spelled the end of alliances and
spheres of influence has scarcely withstood the test of time. Multilateral diplomacy proved no escape from the harsh and morally

127

ambiguous necessities of great power relationships. By the 1950s, the problems of diplomacy in a goldfish bowl were being discussed by dedicated internationalists such as Canada's Lester Pearson and the American scholar, Hans J. Morgenthau. At this time, too, leaders of the so-called uncommitted states in the Cold War such as Nehru, Tito, and Nasser, and representatives of some of the smaller states were calling on the great powers to negotiate, whether within or outside the United Nations. President Dwight D. Eisenhower, spurred on by senior leaders in the Senate, let it be known he was prepared to meet Soviet leader Ñikita Khrushchev for negotiations "at the summit." The concept of "summit diplomacy" has its roots in Winston S. Churchill's repeated arguments for a meeting between leaders of East and West at the highest level and his urgings that a supreme effort be made to bridge the gulf between the nuclear powers that stood on the brink of mutual destruction. (Of course, personal meetings between rulers in an era of aristocratic elites has been common throughout history, and Churchill's knowledge of history undergirded his proposals. Napoleon's meeting with Alexander I at Tilsit is but one especially notable example. Thus Churchill, when he called for a "parley at the summit" in his election speech of February 15, 1950, was not inventing a new concept, but merely proposing the revival of an old practice.) And Secretary of State Henry Kissinger was the architect of what observers have called a diplomacy of movement, making use of the techniques of shuttle diplomacy in the Middle East and Africa.

A list of diplomatic techniques that includes traditional diplomacy, multilateral diplomacy, summit diplomacy, and shuttle diplomacy suggests some of the alternatives from which present and future administrations must choose. The temptation is to assume that the latest is the best, or that principles and problems which apply to one are not relevant to the others. Although this may satisfy certain ingrained needs for reassurance that the nation and its leaders are following a course designed to produce the best of all possible worlds, each form of diplomacy has its peculiar strengths and weaknesses. Moreover, the pursuit of any one brings the diplomatist face to face with troublesome questions that have confounded his predecessors throughout our history. Among them are the issues of:

Secrecy. Within a democracy, few appeals to public opinion are better calculated to provoke response. In the words of the youth movement of the late 1960s, each of us wants a piece of the action, and nothing offends us more than a sense that actions with far-reaching consequences are being taken behind our backs. A feeling of unease sweeps over a local community when too many issues of a city council or school board are settled in executive sessions. The 1976 presidential election may have demonstrated that an updated version of "open covenants openly arrived at" continues to stir the people. But its application has occasioned widespread criticism of Jimmy Carter and the ultimate abandonment of the policy at the Camp David Summit.

Students of diplomacy, if not the people, have turned away from the all-or-nothing character of Woodrow Wilson's formula. Holding to the goal of "open covenants," the revisionists speak disapprovingly of their being privately arrived at. We have returned instead to Walter Lippmann's principle—that individuals can negotiate, but not the people or a public assembly. At the international level, it remained for that consummate negotiator, Dag Hammarskjöld, to draw the United Nations away from kleig-light diplomacy, wherein nations take irreconcilable public positions for the record, toward the practice of quiet diplomacy. As most of us know from family and community disputes, premature open debate is more likely to exacerbate than to resolve deep-seated differences. The private pursuit of conflict management may serve as a poultice to draw out some of the rancor and bitterness of disputes and allow the parties to save face by trade-offs and reformulated objectives that leave vital interests intact.

Deception. It is a commonplace to speak of the diplomat as a man sent abroad to lie and deceive in the interests of his country. The symbol of British diplomacy was Perfidious Albion, and success stories in the history of diplomacy are not generally associated with the work of righteous and morally scrupulous leaders.

To this the great British student of diplomacy, the late Harold Nicolson, replied that lies, half-truths, and deception were a necessary part of the diplomat's strategies and tactics. Yet the diplomat, in Nicolson's words, must return to negotiate another day. A nexus of mutual trust and confidence is vital to the continued processes of diplomacy. It is all too tempting to chronicle the rise and fall of particular diplomats in terms of deception. From Bismarck to Kissinger, the evidence is clear that negotiations sometimes demand saying different things to different leaders. In the words of an historian of the Cold War, Louis J. Halle, "If . . . it is a valid moral principle that one should always speak truthfully, anyone who adhered to that principle literally and invariably, without regard for the practical consequences, would thereby cause all sorts of confusion, entailing bad feeling and perhaps disaster."[5] But there are limits, and deception practiced for deception's sake can undermine a diplomat's capacity to negotiate with others.

Personalism. One of the recurrent concerns of Western diplomats during the Khrushchev era in Soviet foreign policy was that the future of the world depended too much on one man. What if on the eve of a summit conference Khrushchev suffered a stroke? Or what if he were negative because he had eaten a poor breakfast? The first requirement of successful diplomacy has always been that the personal and subjective factor should be filtered out and that negotiations should register in hard print the objective interests of states. In recent decades, there has been a drift away from the objective to the subjective, an increasing stress on the personal and complicating problems resulting from the rise and fall of an individual's personal popularity.

In our third century, whatever the forms of diplomacy employed, a major issue will be the manner in which the problems of secrecy, deception, and personalism are dealt with and incorporated in diplomatic approaches. These issues are central; each arises in varying degrees for those who speak for every pattern of diplomatic relations among states.

3. THE THIRD WORLD AND DEMOCRACY   If the second century was the era in which the Western world responded to the challenge of totalitarianism, the third century may be the time for testing rela-

tions with the Third World. The United States finds itself in the unenviable position of being both defender and scapegoat in the rise of new nations. The billion or more formerly subject peoples who now know independence from colonial regimes owe their freedom, at least in part, to strong postwar American anticolonialism. There are points of moral and political convergence between the United States and the Third World that stem in part from our being present at the creation of the new nations. We and they continue to enjoy common bonds of friendship, as well as mutual interests in education, science, agriculture, and human rights. Their leaders are graduates of our universities; our values, beliefs, and institutions are a part of their heritage. The leaders of their national revolutions have invoked Western traditions and ideas, such as national self-determination and equality, in order to justify themselves to the world. Third World leaders judge their institutions and practices by Western standards, as is exemplified when the educators of Tanzania find fault with their country's higher-education system because of the limited opportunities for women or when African politicians speak out against elitism in African higher education. Inherited educational structures and patterns of governance are necessarily undergoing far-reaching adaptations to bring them into line with African needs; but not infrequently this struggle is taking place through democratic processes within an established institutional framework, especially in education. It would be squandering a rich heritage of common interests to denounce all Third World countries as having fallen permanently into the antidemocratic, authoritarian camp.

At the same time, the less-developed countries are caught in the throes of a choice between order and national survival on one hand and socially worthy goals such as equality and liberty on the other. Not alone for Third World countries, but for nations and peoples everywhere the clash between order and freedom or justice is perennial. If one value and one value only could be the lodestone of conduct, how simple life would be. But values cluster and compete: freedom and order, liberty and justice, the rights of individuals and national security. It serves no one's interest to ignore the terrible predicament men face in having to choose between them.

In the first quarter of the twentieth century, optimism was strong that democracy was on the march. Woodrow Wilson, addressing the Senate on January 22, 1917, could say of American democratic principles: "They are the principles of mankind and must prevail." By the third quarter of the century, Third World leaders were announcing that Western parliamentary democracy was unsuited to their needs. Not democrats but tyrants seemingly prevailed—some benevolent, others social reformers, many better educated than their countrymen. Some now take their inspiration from the West, others are the children of traditional oligarchies, and still others are weaving together strands of Western and anti-Western thought.

For the third century of American foreign policy, three approaches to the Third World are open to the United States. The first is the one which prevailed in the last half of 1975, in which American spokesmen denounced nondemocratic states from the pulpit of the United Nations. Although this may warm the hearts of American nationalists, constitute good electoral politics, and serve to right the record when Third World leaders seek to make the United States the scapegoat for all their ills, it does little to bolster the fragile common interests uniting us with Africa and Latin America. It runs a grave risk of substituting a new Cold War for the one that East and West have so recently brought under some measure of control.

A second approach is to say, with Reinhold Niebuhr, that in every state, including those of the developed world, order precedes liberty and justice. Knowing this, American policy-makers may be better able to deal with nondemocratic states. As a corollary, it may be helpful to consider a distinction, from Guglielmo Ferrerro in his *Principles of Power*, not between democratic and nondemocratic, but between legitimate and illegitimate governments. The legitimate government derives authority from explicit or implicit consent of the governed; illegitimate government, according to Ferrerro, rules only by "force and fraud." Both democratic and traditional governments fall into the category of legitimate governments if we make use of this distinction, for traditional governments rest on implicit consent.

A third approach to Third World governments is to recognize that it is beyond our power to reshape these governments; the most

132

we can hope is that time and patience will lead to healthful changes. This approach is responsive to Halle's warning: "The widespread opinion in the United States that it knows what is best for the rest of the world, that it knows best how to solve the problems of other countries, has caused it to become dangerously overextended since the war, both morally and intellectually with consequences that have manifested themselves most dramatically in Vietnam."[6]

4. GLOBAL HUMAN SURVIVAL   As the United States directs its attention in its third century to world leadership, diplomatic techniques, and the Third World, a still greater challenge remains before it. What are American leaders to say and do about problems of global human survival and the structure of peace? The Indonesian diplomat and historian Soedjatmoko has written:

> We may be only at the beginning of a fundamental redistribution of power across the globe, within nations, and across national boundaries. . . . We are doing so in a world in which no single nation alone is capable of directing and shaping the flow of events . . . and in which most governments . . . seem to be incapable of coming to grips with the problems of their own societies and the anxieties of their citizens. . . . The question we all seem to be facing is whether through impotence or ignorance we allow this fragmented world to be blown up or to drift into destructive chaos and violence, or whether we will be able to move together towards a humane global society.[7]

The problem of global human survival arises in part from man's ignorance of worldwide issues and in his impotence in formulating solutions to the problems he does perceive. Mankind apparently has the means to feed the world, but hunger and poverty remain the permanent condition of hundreds of millions of people in large areas on the globe. We have the most advanced techniques of increasing and transmitting knowledge, but the number of illiterates is growing both in relative and absolute terms. We know more than ever about human nature and unsatisfied human needs; but anxiety and despair, violence and the means of destruction appear to be increasing. We have more data on the requirements of economic growth, but development has not arrested the despoiling of the environment or

133

improved the quality of life. Again, quoting Soedjatmoko: "For those poorer countries which . . . will have to live for a long period at very low income levels, there is the problem of how to organize their societies and their lives in ways which still make it possible to have a meaningful and relatively satisfactory life. In other words, what does quality of life mean to a human being at the level of 100 to 200 dollars per capita per year?"[8]

It is vital to global human survival to give more thought to connections between the expansion of knowledge and the social purposes knowledge can be made to serve. It is important to understand the links between a society's fund of knowledge, its culture, and its dynamics as a whole. If we are to have any future leadership role, we will have to enlarge our capacity for understanding different conditions of life and different modes of living.

All this, however, is not an end in itself, but a means of global human survival. Detente or some form of the reduction of tension between the major powers is one aspect of this quest. In addition, in Ambassador Soedjatmoko's words:

> It will be necessary to defuse the North/South conflict, the growing tensions between the industrial world and the poor pre-industrial countries. Unless that happens, interdependence [which is a two-edged sword] may lead to heightened conflict and wars. There is clear need for the kind of understanding and statesmanship that can move the problems we will have to face away from confrontational rhetoric, away from the frustrations and the anxieties that lie behind the neo-nationalism and the irritation and aggressiveness that characterize so much of the present international dialogue.[9]

Interdependence has become part of official rhetoric in the United States, but it has scarcely penetrated the deeper layers of national consciousness. Contacts by the great powers with the weaker and smaller nations have been mainly on the formers' terms. Most nations have learned early in their history the limits of their security and power; but the United States, with abundant human and material resources, has come late to this discovery. Today a nation, however powerful, cannot solve its problems or define its security in isolation from other nations, great or small.

The route to global human survival is not only through novel international institutions, but through new functional relationships and persuasion, negotiation and bargaining to forge new patterns of international cooperation. If these are some of the means to a global society, so are new visions of the convergence of long-term national interests and a new international order. We must break our present stereotypes about international understanding. We need to delve much more deeply into the cultural substrata of other societies, in which their values, aspirations, fears, ideological perspectives, and motivations to political and social action may be found. It remains to ask what role universities and education can play in all this. Again quoting from Soedjatmoko, here is one far-reaching, if not revolutionary, proposal:

> In the coming decade we may have to consider seriously, building a university capability for global development, either through the restructuring of our universities or through grafting onto existing structures—but fully integrated—academic centers for global development linked together across the globe through formal and informal networks. These centers should not be discipline oriented but should be organized around the major problem areas. . . . Each problem area should be handled by a university division, comprising several disciplines, but at the same time cutting through the more traditional lines of compartmentalization of the university. Food production and distribution, including fertility behavior and population movement . . . resource management and environmental care . . . but also areas dealing with the need in both industrial and developing countries for energy-conserving modes of social organization and personal life styles . . . might be some of these problem areas. The study of these problems should encompass their technological, political, as well as their human dimensions . . . and they should be dealt with on the national level of each nation as well as on the international one.[10]

If all this suggests an educational utopia and an impossible educational dream, it nevertheless points one pathway to global human survival. There may be other and better routes, and surely these ought to attract our best thinking as we move into our third century.

Values and Education:
A Worldwide Review

In the 1940s and 1950s it was fashionable to say that education and
public policy had nothing to do with values; value-free social science held the field and seemed to be the only objective and scientific approach to the great issues of the time. Those who contested
this view were at best a minority; they only gradually found their
way into positions of influence and leadership. Some—like political
philosopher Leo Strauss—rallied followers and founded schools of
thought. But others remained lone scholars whose writings at most
were a modest counterweight to the dominant behavioral science
school. The Ford Foundation in the 1940s and through much of the
1950s concentrated its social science assistance on behaviorism, and
some extraordinarily able and vigorous men participated. Bernard
Berelson, who was to become president of the Population Council,
was a pivotal figure, as were social scientists at Yale and Harvard.
The Rockefeller Foundation had a more-limited focus—concentration on assistance to the pioneering work of Carl Hovland at Yale,
V. O. Key at Harvard, Paul Lazarfeld at Columbia, and the Michigan group including Rensis Likert and Angus Campbell, who looked
at consumer and voter behavior as a particular expression of behavioral science. Because the latter foundation took a more modest
stance and made fewer claims, the reaction, when it came, to the
superiority of the new approaches was less sweeping and devastating in its effects. Significantly, it was the natural and biological
scientists in dominant staff positions at the foundations who expressed early skepticism and held the movement within bounds.
Perhaps they *understood* what others had to *discover*—that science
has both immense possibilities and rather severe limitations.

I recite the foundations' experience because I was a part of the
Thermidorean reaction when it came, and I observed and influenced
the change. The foundations are a rather accurate barometer of the
sense of the country at large, though there are often points of rigidity
and overkill built into their response. The growing sense of discontent began with men of affairs: Raymond Fosdick, Robert Lovett,

Dean Rusk, Henry Alan Moe, Henry Pitt Van Dusen, Robert Loeb, Ralph Bunche, Chester Bowles, and others. They knew firsthand that any tidy separation of thought into facts and values had little relationship to reality. However convenient, this approach bore little resemblance to experience, and they challenged "behaviorism" first on this front. Their counterattack had roots in other soil, and they were, if anything, more outspoken there. These men, without exception, knew that "man does not live by bread alone." The compelling force of social and political ideas could not be explained by any narrow calculus of stimulus and response. Understanding social and political coherence and the partly irrational dynamics of politics required more than social surveys and election studies. Loyalties, commitments, and decisions had perplexed and preoccupied these men of action. They were impatient with those who cast these rich and varied phenomena in an oversimplified behavioral mold. They also turned away from scholars who rejected the study of important problems for more trivial concerns that were susceptible to new methods of testing and counting. A favorite analogy drawn from the writings of Arnold J. Toynbee was an account of an inebriated Englishman discovered under a lamppost. Asked by a policeman about his intention, he explained that he had lost his watch. The bobby asked if he had lost the watch near the lamppost. No, came the answer, he had dropped it in a darkened alley. Why then wasn't he searching for it there? Because there was light only under the lamppost. Methodology has imposed its own laws and priorities; it, and not the problem, was accountable for the agenda for study and led inescapably toward society's knowing more and more about less and less. Ignoring what is most significant is the core of the indictment.

This led men like Fosdick, Lovett, Rusk, Bunche, Moe, and a former dean of the Wharton School of Business, then director of the Social Sciences Division of the Rockefeller Foundation, Joseph H. Willits, to launch a program encouraging serious study of moral and political philosophy. It was at its height a modest venture, involving no large institutional grants but only the support of some exceptional individuals. A few dedicated staff officers, such as Columbia

137

University's Herbert Deane and Barnard College's John B. Stewart,
were commissioned to set out in search, not for Diogenes' "honest
man," but for scholars and observers concerned with values. The
lonely individual was pushed to the fore; men like John Plamanetz,
H. L. A. Hart, John Rawls, Michael Oakeshott, and Reinhold Niebuhr
became subjects of attention comparable in importance to large-scale
social survey centers. In some small measure, the tide turned. Thinking and willing became as important as counting. Values supplanted
voting as a primary concern, and years later Dean Rusk was to say
that support of individual scholars in legal, moral, and political
philosophy headed the list of social science programs during his
tenure as president of the Rockefeller Foundation.

1. VALUES AND EDUCATION The approaches to the problem of values were directed primarily at areas of law, society, and politics in
the Rockefeller program. The trustees were persuaded that these
areas comprised the sphere in which the dilemmas of moral choice
were most acute. For it was here that the claims of freedom and
order, liberty and equality, justice and power hung in the balance. In
no other sphere were the stakes as high. The issue was nothing less
than survival. Other sectors paled in significance compared with law
and politics.

It was not long, however, before such a narrow conception of
ethics yielded to reality. The arena for law and politics was broader
than the courtroom and parliament. The dramas of most lasting importance were played out in the community, the churches, and the
schools. It was here that groups contended and cooperated, rules and
laws worked themselves out, and justice or injustice prevailed. Education is one of the several broad areas for which value analysis is
essential.

The value question manifests itself at many points in education,
but nowhere more vividly than with regard to purpose. It is axiom-
atic, given the passions that control men's actions, that survival is
a race between education and destruction. Yet to restate this leaves
unanswered the question: "Education for what?" The Germans under Hitler were a highly cultured people who wreaked destruction

on the world; Americans have suffered pangs of conscience since the bombings of Hiroshima and Nagasaki, as well as over our role in the Vietnam War.

The real issue turns, then, on the meaning and purposes of education, not its existence or institutionalization alone. We link education in liberal democratic societies to what we call the open society, to liberating the minds of citizens on whom survival depends. The educated man must be emancipated from the tyrannies that make him insensitive to alternatives and blind him to consequences. Men are born free, but live everywhere in chains—cribbed and confined by ancient creeds and doctrines. The educated man must be an agent of change and an instrument of progress. Man finds himself in a world rent by social and biological revolutions, sweeping alternations in national and interpersonal moods. He has less time to ponder, more choices to make; and these choices are made in an angry, restless, impatient world. It is more difficult to forgive and forget than to practice restraint. Life-styles have changed, and there are far-reaching perplexities about who we are and where we are going. Through it all, man's questions outnumber his answers. From a doctrineless position, he has little way of discerning and distinguishing the enduring from the transient, the timeless from the mere passions of the present. Modern man has witnessed the demise of the nineteenth-century idea of unending progress. He would like to believe that certain worldwide forces are driving mankind toward a higher moral plane—but too often this is challenged by the evidence.

Thus, thinking about social and educational issues, man is pushed back to ancient truths. He turns to recent but premodern thought expressed by William James: "It is not thinking with its primitive ingenuity of childhood that is difficult, but to think with tradition, with all its acquired force." He turns back to such classical distinctions as the necessary, the possible, and the best. Some would say that the aphorism "the best is the enemy of the good" is self-evident, no more than a vulgar truism out of phase with the ethos of the time. The 1960s and 1970s have taught, however, that responsibility must be the handmaiden of freedom. At least some of our educational thinkers have rediscovered education for responsibility,

which presupposes both process and purpose. Openness itself must
be grounded on some form of commitment, whether to science, progress, or truth. Man can afford to be open only because he has
moorings and bench marks, and it is not enough to take these for
granted. Assumptions must be made explicit, and value premises as
well as social predictions must continually be held up to scrutiny
and review.

If we move from high principle and general truths, we confront
the need for operational values that touch the question of "education
for what?" For the United States and the developed countries and, in
the long run, for developing countries, four necessarily oversimple
propositions and guidelines present themselves.

First, education must attend both to individual and collective
needs. While fostering such aims as individualism and equal opportunity, it must help to give a social and political identity, a sense of
who we are as a people and as a part of mankind. When we were less
knit together by technology and communications, we could afford to
have many nations within the one, with different levels of opportunity and citizenship. Today a house divided simply cannot stand.
This may be a counsel toward perfection, but it is also a guide to
survival. The stress in the 1970s is on cultural pluralism and ethnic
diversity; talk of e pluribus unum may appear quaint and old-fash-
ioned. It happens, however, to be the bedrock on which the American republic is founded. (Other republics, too, rest on a similar
bedrock.)

The struggle for equality for individuals and groups is always
socially disrupting; it feeds on a certain dynamic and momentum.
We jostle one another as we seek equality. Those who are asked to
share privilege and power do well to call up Marianne Moore's telling phrase, "One is not rich but poor, when one can always seem so
right." Both those who give and suffer provocation may take comfort; change and growth bring contradictions and schism. Every action and counteraction has its price. The end of the story in periods
of change is seldom the event. It would give us strength and ultimate
unity if we could say, with Miss Moore, "The deepest feeling shows
itself in silence," or, as she then added, "not silence but restraint."

However utopian—and there are Americans such as President Abraham Lincoln who have followed such counsel—these words might help peoples to discover, whatever their differences, that they also share deep-running tides of unity which strident popular debate can but temporarily obscure.

Secondly, education needs to avoid the apocalyptic view. Martin Luther's affirmation has a continuing relevance: "Even if I were told that the world was going to pieces tomorrow, I would still plant my apple tree today and pay my debts." Yet this may be asking too much of contemporary men and societies. In personal and national life, we are regularly driven to the precipice of despair, so continuous and all-consuming are the crises we face. In the 1960s, the watchword was "the new man" and, failing that, "the apocalypse." To live with problems and hammer out approaches sufficient to the day has little appeal, especially to the young. Yet in 1979 the new man does not walk among us, the radicals like Eldridge Cleaver have repented, and total and comprehensive solutions are not in sight.

Thirdly, education should not scorn, but should help us return to the marketplace, for we suffer grievously from the lack of improved machinery for public and private decision-making. The trouble both with silent majorities or marching minorities is that while they are silent or marching, someone else moves in, grasps power, makes the decisions. It is not participation as aimless and noisy activity that is needed; nor will self-righteous factionalism, which almost always divides and destroys, suffice. It is participation exerting leverage on policy with the aim of acting responsibly. The warning of Dietrich Bonhoeffer, the great German theologian and resistance leader, should be writ large on the banners of every activist group: "It is easier to act on abstract principle than from concrete responsibility." And those who strive to do this must immerse themselves in matters, however limited, wherein they have earned the right to be heard.

Fourthly, education which would truly serve mankind and be faithful to enduring values requires concrete and definable targets. In the developing world, it must help men cope with population control, produce more food, curb inflation, improve the environment, limit and contain conflict, enhance public health, train for jobs

141

and employment, and then start all over by preparing to meet the
next challenge. The mandate is to help and serve, not presume to
have the answers. None of these steps will bring about a new world.
Taken together, there is a chance they will contribute. As Jonathan
Swift wrote in *Gulliver's Travels* (which has special relevance to
our day): "And he gave it as his opinion that whoever could make
two ears of corn, or two blades of grass, to grow upon a spot of
ground where only one grew before, would deserve better of mankind, and do more essential service to his country, than the whole
race of politicians put together."[11] It would be hard to state the
moral grounds for feeding mankind or responding to fundamental
human needs in more eloquent terms.

Thus education which would turn from mechanics to values
needs operational guidelines. It has to link actions and purpose,
change and continuity, institutions and human values. But it must
do more than this. With Alfred North Whitehead, it must realize that
the first step of wisdom is recognizing that the major advances in
civilization are processes that can rend society. Without combining
reverence for symbols with freedom to revise those symbols, societies will decay. The demands of society are too great to allow men
to choose between the old and the new. Ancient symbols and their
revision are the necessary parts of an approach to the whole.

2. EDUCATION IN THE DEVELOPING COUNTRIES   A good laboratory
for studying values and education is the Third World, in which the
struggle to relate values and education is being fought out. The
twelve-donor agency study of higher education, discussed in Chapter III, pp. 61ff, arose from a sense of disillusionment in many of the
agencies. It was argued, sometimes vociferously, that higher education had contributed little to the most urgent needs of the developing
world. Too many Third World institutions were carbon copies of
Western universities. Local educators had slavishly imitated French,
British, Dutch, or American models; friends who came bearing gifts
had been all too willing to accept the subservience of those who
sought their aid. The aid that had been given over a twenty-five-year
period had been largely wasted. Disenchantment, coupled with the
desire to do something new and more fashionable, was pushing

some agencies toward new areas, leaving higher education "to stew in its own juice." On the human side, some of the leaders who had championed aid to higher education were stepping aside. Nevertheless, there were signs of other agencies experiencing a resurgence of interest, as in the willingness of USAID to contemplate doing more.

At one level, agency disillusionment was unjustified and misplaced. Forgotten was the youthfulness of Third World higher education, especially in Africa. University education in Europe, by comparison, goes back to the eleventh century. Most new universities are in their infancy, having a decade or less of experience. Moreover, the newly independent countries find themselves under the weight of strong nationalistic compulsion. Just as they are obliged to demonstrate that they can provide for their own national security, they are under compulsion to show themselves capable of building quality universities. In almost every African country, therefore, the creation of an elitist university comes first, for the same reason that a national airline is a sign of national prestige. Viewed more positively, these institutions are the means of training, as rapidly as possible, cadres of civil servants and faculties for other institutions throughout the land.

The twelve-donor agency study, however, throws into question certain widely held notions in the West. Practically none of the twenty-three institutions studied fit the stereotype of ivory-tower universities. Most are deeply committed to development aims. To claim universality for a modest sample of Third World institutions would be wrong. The selection process was weighted toward studying institutions that were doing something about the needs of their people and were innovative in their approach. No one can say how representative they are or how readily their numbers could be increased. What seems indisputable is the fact that at least twenty institutions are directing an important part of their educational effort to such central problems as increasing food production, building better health delivery systems, orienting education to the needs of both the rural and urban poor, and improving the rest of the educational system. In this they are expressing a value preference that may be as important as the efficiency of their work.

As I have noted, Third World educators made the selection and

143

themselves conducted the case studies. More noteworthy still, the group passed over some of the premiere, best-known institutions in their regions. In part such choices were affected by the quest for institutions that were serving as engines of change. With due allowance for this, the fact remains that "insiders" made choices which differed somewhat from those that would have been made by "outsiders" from external agencies. This prompted the proposal that external groups should lean more on local wisdom, along with new style mechanisms for bilateral and multilateral aid combining local and outside representatives.

There is much evidence of the need for operational principles relating values to education in the case studies. In almost every institution, attention to the individual and the group was stressed. Pressures to build national identity have their effects. When the goals of the nation are preeminent, as in Tanzania, individuals are forced into a mold. Their development comes second to national development or, put more felicitously, the two must be made to converge. Young people seeking admission to the University of Dar es Salaam must prove their social commitment by working for a year or more beside workers and peasants between secondary and higher education. Their loyalty to the social revolution is judged not by academic performance but by their living and working with the people. To use the economist's vocabulary, those who judge such a system must measure the trade-offs between individual fulfillment and service to the wider good.

Sometimes the struggle to balance the rights of the individual and those of the group involved the matter of tribalism. All through its early history, the University of Ibadan in Nigeria reflected the influence and ability of the Ibos. Following the Nigerian Civil War, the Ibos were supplanted by Yoruba faculty and staff, and excellence was equated with the political dominance of the western tribal group. The same conflict between particular and fragmentary interests and groups continues in Malaysia, where Malays struggle to replace Chinese not only in leadership posts but in quotas of students. The same social turmoil that divides Western institutions is a source of conflict in developing universities.

Secondly, the immediacy of human survival problems has mini-mized the presence of apocalyptic thinking. It may be a telling commentary on human nature that where problems are truly over-whelming, men—and particularly the young—have less time to proclaim the end of the world. Prophets of doom in the developed world are often the well-placed but disillusioned children of middle- and upper-class groups who judge society by the liberal standards their parents espouse in theory and fall short of in practice. Not only are the tasks of society so great that higher standards are out of place, but first-generation revolutionary leaders soon become the defenders of newly acquired privileges and power. Serious challengers to this brand of elitism are yet to appear on the scene. Order must precede freedom and equality; the environment, for a time, favors those struggling to manage an essentially unstable social system.

Thirdly, education in developing countries shares the plight of developed societies seeking to bring educated men and women into the marketplace. In a nutshell, this is what education for develop-ment is all about. Indeed the main thrust of those developing univer-sities which have done most for their societies is pursuit of new patterns of higher education. The risk inherent in this approach is that of substituting one foreign model for another. The twelve-donor agency study found developing country educators as wary of new models as of old. The Latin American team took exception to our describing their development-oriented universities as copies of any others. When I wrote in the final report that the rural university in Peru, La Molina, was a land-grant type university, the group sub-stituted the phrase, "a university seeking to transfer agricultural technologies to middle and small landowners in Peru." It is indis-criminate application of all foreign models to new problems and circumstances that is suspect, not a particular British or American model. The Third World increasingly is taking seriously the dictum that it must indeed act from concrete responsibility rather than any set of abstract principles.

Fourthly, education everywhere, but most of all in the develop-ing world, requires its own well-defined and specific goals and targets. The Western world has shared a rich legacy with the rest of the world by insisting that the first aim of education must be to teach men to think. Educational institutions without standards too soon become diploma mills, selling their wares for profit without integrity or serious purpose. New countries have need of models cast not in a Western mold, but dedicated to historic and time-tested goals. In these terms, the University of Ibadan or the University of Ghana become examples and models for other regional universities that will follow; without them, successor institutions would lack tangible evidence of what a university is or must seek to become.

Institution-building may be the beginning of educational development in the less-developed countries, but it is unlikely to be the end. For the human condition is hedged about with a host of irreducible survival needs: hunger and famine, misery and disease, high infant mortality and low life expectancy, unemployment and underemployment, shortages of resources and capital, poor housing and worse sanitation, too few educational opportunities and rapid population growth. External agencies are able, in programing assistance efforts, to indulge themselves in the luxury of confronting these needs one at a time—now public health, next food production, and only then educational reform. The new countries, balancing precariously on survival's precipice, must grapple with these needs not seriatim but all at once. Responsible national leaders must do something to meet every emerging need or their publics will turn to others, often on the far right or far left, however false and inflated their promises.

For these reasons, the emergence of strong new programs devoted to urgent needs have importance far exceeding institution-building. It is of the greatest importance in Africa that the University of Yaoundé in Cameroon, under the tutelage of the extraordinarily able Dr. G. L. Monekosso, has developed its equivalent of a "barefoot doctors" approach to rural health problems. Auxiliaries and technicians are trained alongside medical doctors in the university of Yaoundé's health sciences center and sent as health teams to deprived rural areas. Across the Atlantic, on the western coast of South America, two dedicated Colombian surgeons, in partnership with two private American foundations, fashioned a new approach to health delivery that reached disadvantaged urban and rural areas in the Cauca Valley of Colombia and in the process infused the University of Valle with a powerful new ethos. In the mid-1970s one of these leaders moved to the Federal University of Bahia to test whether what was done in Colombia could be extended to Brazil. Seven of the institutions in the twelve-donor agency study are grappling with the multiple problems of the poor, including food and nutrition, health and sanitation, and housing. Three are focusing on health, six on improving teacher training, and six on manpower training.

From all these educational experiments, lessons have been learned on structure, planning, leadership, and government relations. And a highly tentative set of guidelines on principles of education for development is now at hand. And in every case evidence multiplies that traditional educational structures may often be a prime obstacle to service to the community. Patterns of governance that lodge decision-making authority in senates and councils, copying older Western institutions, obstruct innovation and change. In Brazil, the system of a single professor for each discipline, the *cathedratico*, weights the decision-making process strongly in favor of the status quo and drives innovators outside the established system. The price of working outside the system, of course, is to deny leading institutions the strengthening and enrichment that comes from basic teaching and research. The new universities at their best ought to strive to respond to urgent human needs without rejecting the traditional goals of education—advancing and diffusing knowledge, educating for citizenship, forming values, fulfilling individual aspirations, and training developers to meet the needs of society. On this there has been significant unanimity, both in the developing countries and among developed country advisors.

3. UNIVERSITIES AND SOCIAL VALUES The value problem cuts deeper than the accomplishments, however striking, of developing country institutions. It goes to the heart of the relationship between the social values of a nation and the life and work of its universities. On the one hand, universities may reflect the controlling values of a society or more often the values of whatever group may be dominant

in that society. On the other hand, the relationship may be one of tension between those who control the university and society at large. There may be a gulf, whether ideological or ethnic, between those who govern society and those who govern the university. Mass opinion may be pushing society in one direction, whereas university thinking turns it toward other ends. A further tension develops when universities engage in development planning; for even when there is consensus on ends, dissension on means may obtain: who does the planning, what students are admitted to the university, and who shapes their attitudes and values?

The history of colonial education in many developing countries illustrates the point. Institutions were seldom an outgrowth of indigenous cultures; in a dual sense, they were transplants as institutional structures and as expressions of underlying value systems. Their outward forms were those of residential colleges with all the trappings, but more profoundly they imported goals and values corresponding to those of the colonial powers. Not by accident were they elitist in character, because their product was to be an indigenous elite, willing and able to take on the values and duties of the colonial administrators with whom they were to work and whom they were eventually to replace. Curricula and fields of study were carefully chosen and tailored to this end. Law and political science found their way into universities late in the day, but public administration and some aspects of medical science were important instruments for maintaining a colonial order. Colonial universities, moreover, were relatively immune to the radicalizing influences universities in the United Kingdom and France were likely to foster. It was in the best colonial interest, therefore, to build indigenous universities to guard against the phenomenon of nationalist leaders—as in the case of Kwame Nkrumah—being infected with a Western liberal or radical virus.

The result was the forming of an administrative and educational elite, skilled in the techniques of management and control, broadly versed in Western history and culture, but almost totally divorced from the thinking and feeling of their own people. Only gradually and by dint of the insistence of men of exceptional intellectual powers were native subjects "imported" into the curriculum. It required someone as formidable as Kenneth O. Dike, now professor of African history at Harvard University and formerly vice chancellor of the University of Ibadan, to establish the study of African history at Ibadan. A scheme of "special lectureships" initiated by an American foundation paved the way for young Africans to remain at the University of East Africa until establishment posts, especially in new subjects, were created. With national independence, no group of indigenous leaders moved into positions of high administrative responsibility more effectively than did the products of this colonial regime. They had, however, been uprooted from their own cultures; their social and cultural interests had become Western, not local; their standards of living sometimes eclipsed their expatriate predecessors; they held to the perquisites of office in countries whose per capita incomes hovered near the margin of survival. No one can ever detract from the educational achievements of the colonial rulers in training top leaders, but they were leaders referred to by some of their compatriots with various pejorative terms such as "Afro-Saxons."

With independence, the new universities seeking to become more authentic had two alternatives. They could continue the traditions inherited from the colonial power, adapting and modifying them, in effect nationalizing them to harmonize with local needs. Or they could create new institutions. The older universities—Delhi, University of the Philippines and the University of Ghana—were able to do this because university values were compatible with those of the new ruling elite. When the ruling elite had different values, as exemplified in the socialist goals of Tanzania, the inherited values of the university became an obstacle to the building of a socialist society. Therefore, the University of Dar es Salaam from its creation was a departure from Makerere (Uganda) and Ibadan. It began with a law faculty, embraced political science, and recast its curriculum in an African mold. Even here, there was give and take between inherited traditions, which had gone largely unquestioned in older institutions, and new national goals. The quest for distinctive new institutions is a more complex and painful process than maintaining the

149

old, and such institutions seek help wherever they can find it. At Dar es Salaam, Canadians, Scandinavians, and East Europeans joined British and American scholars to formulate the new curricula. The inherited tradition became eclectic, drawing on diverse national experiences which Tanzanians sought to synthesize into a new socialist educational system.

Building the curriculum, complex as this may be and as subject to controversy and debate, hardly compares to the efforts to transform student attitudes and values in the Third World. National service in Tanzania, advice to farmers in Peru, rural health projects in Colombia and Cameroon, and rural education programs in northern Nigeria and Ethiopia—all are designed to sensitize students to urgent human needs and thereby transform the values of society. New courses on national history and rural problems are directed to similar ends. Some developing universities recognize both the intrinsic merit of understanding traditional culture and the residual political power of traditional oligarchs. Such steps, then, are designed to close the gap between the so-called modern universities and the traditional sector of their societies. For students seeking to escape the misery of their native culture, they may smack of social engineering; and yet they are obvious measures known in so-called free societies to build loyalties that are judged essential to the future both of the universities and the societies on which they depend.

The real issue for developing universities arises when they must make a choice between supporting and reinforcing the dominant values of society or challenging and opposing them. The choice is one that the academic man cannot escape. At one level, it is the choice between theory and practice, or philosophy and action. It presents conflicts of values, which process is all too familiar in the West. In developing countries, the conflict is more severe and involves whole institutions. So interconnected are government and universities that the choice may amount to declaring intellectual civil war within a country. Any such choice is fraught with the gravest moral and economic consequences. It involves moral and political judgment and discrimination of the highest order. University leaders operate within the narrowest of constraints, and open persecution is ever feared as a response by public authority to their protests.

It is a choice that men such as Alex Kwapong, then vice chancellor of the University of Ghana, had to make in the Nkrumah period. Here it involved, at most, quiet resistance to total political control. A similar choice within narrow limits is the one confronting university leaders at Makerere University in Uganda today. It occurs as well in certain South African universities in which liberal and humanistic values clash with the dominant values of the state. A modernizing university that introduces more rational and scientific approaches to society's needs may find itself in conflict with traditional oligarchs opposing change.

Historically, the university in the West has been a citadel for social criticism, a force for independent thinking insulated from public passions. The story is told of President Robert Hutchins of the University of Chicago, who dealt directly with legislative and business leaders who criticized the thinking of individual professors. Hutchins often met the criticism himself, never troubling the professors with the hostile views and letters emanating from outside the university. Only years later did the faculty members learn what he had done. One has only to ask to what extent this approach would be possible in the developing countries to note the difference. Professors in Chilean universities today face the prospect of imprisonment when they criticize the state, and Chile's predicament is not an isolated one. When the crisis is fundamental, the university's role must nevertheless be one of beleaguered champion against oppression— an heroic position in which individuals must be ready to pay the price. The first principal of the University of Dar es Salaam has written: "There will be some situations in which universities in the Third World ... [must] assist the processes of social change being promoted by their governments and ... others where they should ... stand aside ... bearing witness to alternative values and providing a base for informed and critical analysis of these efforts." [12]

Facing the problem of choice, Third World educators must make value judgments. Universities cannot avoid them. They have a responsibility to their societies and the whole intellectual community.

151

They cannot be ethically neutral, and the rub comes when they must be concrete.

So we return to the point at which we began. A value-free social science is of little worth to developing country educators. They must find ways of distinguishing their role, say, at the National University of Chile under the Frei regime from that under the present military government. No serious thinker has ever claimed that moral choices are easy. Nor should anyone suppose that value judgments are free of consequences. The point is to recognize, with responsible educators, that in developed or in Third World countries, choices must be made. Moral reasoning, with its ancient and respected tradition, is as vital to education as to every other area of society.

Conclusions

The study and discussion of ethics, functionalism, and power would represent a worthy intellectual challenge if foreign policy were nothing more than an exciting adventure in game theory or model-building. Experiments in advancing definitions and refining concepts are not without merit for those who participate. However, foreign policy (as is true of moral choice in individual lives) is far more than an exercise in conceptualizing or problem-solving. For those involved, it can be a matter of life and death. Today it has become a question of global human survival as man, in building weapons of mass destruction, has climbed the steep path toward mutual annihilation. Never before have costs been so great and consequences so serious. Man has the capacity to destroy his universe—and he knows it.

Politically, the world today bears little resemblance to that preceding World War II, and if anyone doubts the extent of change let him attend sessions of the General Assembly of the United Nations whose membership has tripled in the past three decades. Yet the achievement of near-universal membership in one world organization has not brought the millennium. Instead it has created a host of new problems and unforeseen opportunities. A vast array of new ministates has discovered in the United Nations a worldwide forum for voicing its grievances without having the power or resources for matching declaration with responsibility. The Maldive Islands and the United States each have one vote to cast in support of their "grand designs," leading one somewhat cynical Western observer to ask whether Stalin in 1945 had not been right in arguing that the Soviet Union deserved multiple votes because of the size of individual Soviet Socialist Republics such as Byelorussia and the Ukraine. Responsibility and power need to be joined, whether in the family or in the world community. Having denied the enduring importance of power in international relations for generations, Americans are now faced within and outside world forums with the necessity of thinking more clearly about relationships between power and responsibility.

Nationalism and nation-states are equated with power at a moment in history when nation-states are no longer able to fulfill all responsibilities of protecting the security and providing for the well-being of large numbers of people. In the present industrial world, the decline in authority of the nation-state (if not its obsolescence) has forced once independent states to turn to larger groupings of nations for safety and prosperity. Great Britain is the one most conspicuous example of a nation which for centuries held itself aloof from the initial stages of European struggles, throwing its weight to one side or the other to preserve the balance of power; but Britain now has joined its destiny with that of Western Europe in a community of European states.

The decline of exclusive nationalism, the diminished authority of the nation-state, and the quest for larger groupings of states in the developed world has not occurred in the same manner or to the same degree in the underdeveloped countries. For them, national loyalties long held in check have exploded with irresistible force and logic. Nationalism has become the one unifying force capable of transcending subnational loyalties—whether ethnic ties, tribal bonds, or former colonial relationships. It has become the cement that gives coherence to often incoherent unions of diverse and disparate peoples. For wider communities, nationalism can present obstacles to cooperation, yet no amount of exhortation by world statesmen seems likely to diminish its influence or wish it away in the Third World.

In this there is a note of tragic irony for liberal and humane

153

Western peacemakers. Woodrow Wilson gave first place to national self-determination among his Fourteen Points for peace; latter-day Wilsonians from Cordell Hull to Daniel P. Moynihan have clung to the tenets of the Wilsonian creed. But not only have the newer nations refused to behave as Wilson prophesied they would, national self-determination' poses its own set of complex problems. (See pp. 130 and 133, herein.) Wilson and his followers had assumed that national self-determination would rest on the will of the people as registered in free elections and plebiscites. However, most of the new African states and Indonesia, to say nothing of some of the states created in East Central Europe after World War I, were not established on the basis of free elections or plebiscites. In many such countries the old colonial boundaries have prevailed. How is national self-determination to be established in the absence of a plebiscite or some other means of determining the will of the people? The establishment of conditions of peace, moreover, has not been uniformly successful even with plebiscites, as evidenced in the case of Austria-Hungary, where a plebiscite was held only in Carinthia and the Slovenes' majority vote demonstrated that they wished to remain with Austria. The natural processes of national self-determination have run afoul of great power politics and ancient rivalries. It would appear that the workings of national self-determination have been subject to constraints that its authors had not fully anticipated.

These issues bring us back to the stubbornly persistent problems of international politics: national fears and rivalries, clashes of national and regional interests, security-power dilemmas and the tragic element in politics. None of these historic questions is absent from the contemporary international scene, however much their forms and patterns may be altered. In the nineteenth century the British statesman George Canning called on the new world to redress the balance of the old world.[13]

Today what may be needed is for classical thought to redress the balance of modern thought, to bring to bear on present-day problems the wisdom of moral and political reasoning. The need for moral reasoning would be less pressing in our day if a single moral and political goal, whether nationalism or world government, could resolve all mankind's problems. The signs are beyond dispute, however, that for nations (as for individuals) purposes and goals cluster and compete. In international politics and morality, there is no one overarching purpose by which all competing purposes can be hierarchically ordered and arranged. The international order continues to be shaped by a pluralism of moral and political purposes, which statesmen must balance or order to fit changing needs and circumstances.

Thus the wisest leaders and thinkers whose words and deeds have enduring value in our time have called for a return to moral reasoning. Prudence has once more become the highest virtue in politics; practical morality which seeks to balance what is morally right with what is politically feasible has become a stark necessity. Justice requires that men and nations relearn in each successive crisis the ever-painful and perplexing art of placing themselves in the position of friend or foe. Prudence is the highest civic virtue, because in politics it is essential not only to strive for justice but also to take into account all the contingencies that determine the peace and well-being of a community or a state. All policies and actions in politics require a shrewd admixture of principles and expediency in their use and loyalty to standards of justice tempered to meet the power political realities of the moment. Questions of relative good and evil are the raw stuff of politics. Political problems are never a mattter of absolute truth or falsehood viewed metaphysically. Principles have to be measured by the concrete harm or good they bring to the community. Historical conditions give every standard of justice its distinguishing color and discriminating effect. What is good is good in proportion to other things, to effects and results. Principles must be weighed in relationship with other principles. The rules of prudence are never exact, seldom universal. They are subject to the dominion of circumstances. Prudence supplies concrete reasons in politics, where abstract principles are insufficient or irrelevant.

The student of international politics, then, must look for relationships, master the facts, weigh power and morality, balance ends and means. If men in modern times have been led by their teachers to believe the search for peace and order is a simple, rational, and mechanical undertaking, they must find their way back to an older tradition of thought. Practical morality remains the best if the most demanding road to follow. Its principles undergird all that has been written in this study of ethics, functionalism, and power. The cornerstone is political realism and practical morality's uniting of what has been said about both the possibilities and limitations of building a structure of peace for nations and the world.

Epilogue

The major outlines of this study reflect my personal and professional experiences and the influences that have shaped my thought. Looking back on what I have written about ethics, functionalism, and power, I feel an obligation to offer a few concluding thoughts. My interest in ethics has had a long if sometimes troubled history. The child of a parsonage, I listened to words about right and wrong from the earliest days of which I have any consciousness. Of more influence, however, than the words were the living examples of two parents who put their stress on deeds. The steadiness of my mother's moral course in every dimension of her living was a constant inspiration. From my parents I learned more about ethics in life than from any amount of reading or reflection. It was also my good fortune to study not with one but with three scholars—professors of English, history, and philosophy—who, whatever the subject, could not conceal their abiding concern with morality and society. In graduate school and after, I fell under the influence of three of the most powerful political thinkers of our times—Hans J. Morgenthau, Reinhold Niebuhr, and Quincy Wright. Whenever I have sensed the need for renewal of my thinking, I have gone back to the writings of these men, especially those of the first two. The years of World War II provided the severest test for anyone who sought to understand ethical issues, but they also helped one to distinguish what had enduring value from what was limited, ephemeral.

World War II also inspired most young Americans to seek out the

157

basis of a more lasting peace. Some of the peace plans that both
young and old embraced proved either illusory or impractical. Yet
the quest for world order was a goal that would persist, and David
Mitrany's *A Working Peace System* offered a more realistic basis for
hope. Functionalism remained an abstraction for me until I was
given an opportunity to serve in the international programs of a large
private American foundation. Here was a realm of America's involvement in foreign countries for which the conventional wisdom
of foreign policy appeared not wholly relevant. Educators, agriculturalists, and public health professionals worked side by side
seemingly without regard for countries of origin. Their intellectual
and scientific journey began with a problem—famine, malnutrition, or
disease. The leaders of the developing countries called on American
or European scientists to help them overcome a crippling need or
deficiency. I repeatedly observed professionals working with professionals—growing a crop or rooting out disease in a manner that
could be explained more fully by functionalism than by power
politics. Yet politics was never too far removed from the national
system within which development efforts went on; and the more
successful a functional experiment in agriculture or health, the more
likely it was that national governments would exercise control or
take the credit. Functionalist theory presupposed that technical
cooperation within an international framework would weaken the
sense of exclusive nationalism and break through national boundaries. I looked for clear and unequivocal signs that this could happen; but, paradoxically, the success stories in international scientific
cooperation within a developing country strengthened bonds among
diverse national professionals working together while heightening
the beneficiary's national pride.

When I returned to the study of diplomatic relations among
nation-states, the primacy of national interest and the struggle for
power was once again apparent. No other theory proved quite so
controling as the one which presupposed that nations put their own
interests first. To assume that philanthropic motives alone could
guide national policy-makers or that service to mankind could be the
touchstone of foreign policy would be illusory. A national leader is

pledged, by oath of office, to safeguard national security. Thus foreign relations, to the objective and dispassionate observer, has many of the same characteristics that have prevailed throughout the history of the European state system. I found I could not study or teach international politics in the same idiom that I had used in trying to explain international cooperation in science or education.

The origins of this volume, then, stem from the fact that I have lived successively and, on occasion simultaneously, in three worlds: as an individual concerned with questions of ethics, as a professional foundation official serving abroad, and as a student of foreign policy. The three worlds are lamentably not the same. Each has its own context, its own requirements. Differing theoretical frameworks would seem appropriate to the different spheres. In a certain sense, each is quite independent of the others.

However, all three come together to interact and influence one another at certain critical points. Each of the three constitutes a part of the international experience. Someday some preeminent thinker will fit them together more fully than I have done into a comprehensive international theory. Until that day, my hope would be that I will at least have demonstrated that ethics, functional cooperation, and power represent important segments of the subject matter of international studies. Regardless of whether they can be fully integrated, they represent the main currents of thought within the broad area of international politics.

Notes

NOTES TO CHAPTER I

1 Washington *Post*, October 31, 1976, Sec. K., p. 1.
2 New York *Times*, January 3, 1973, p. 34.
3 *Ibid.*
4 *Ibid.*
5 *Ibid.*
6 Calvin D. Davis, *The United States and the First Hague Conference* (Ithaca, N.Y.: Cornell University Press, 1962), 213.
7 Calvin D. Davis, *The United States and the Second Hague Conference* (Ithaca, N.Y.: Cornell University Press, 1976), 363.
8 *Ibid.*, 137, 161.
9 New York *Times*, January 3, 1973, p. 34.
10 *Ibid.*, January 4, 1973, p. 37.
11 *Ibid.*, November 19, 1943, p. 1.
12 *Ibid.*
13 *Ibid.*
14 *Ibid.*
15 John Milton, *Complete Prose Works*, ed. Don M. Wolfe (4 vols.; New Haven, Conn.: Yale University Press, 1959), II, 550.
16 Hugo Grotius, *Prolegomena to the Law of War and Peace*, trans. Francis W. Kelsey (New York: Liberal Arts Press, 1957), par. 28.
17 John Bunyan, *Pilgrim's Progress*, ed. James B. Wharey (Oxford: Clarendon Press, 1928), 85.
18 Percy E. Corbett, *Morals, Law and Power in International Relations* (Los Angeles: John Randolph Haynes and Dora Haynes Foundation, 1956), 2.
19 Davis, *Second Hague Conference*, 165.
20 Corbett, *Morals, Law and Power*, 15–16, 50.
21 Charles de Visscher, *Theory and Reality in Public International Law*, trans. Percy E. Corbett (Princeton, N.J.: Princeton University Press, 1957), 99.
22 *Ibid.*, 98.
23 *Ibid.*, xii.
24 Reinhold Niebuhr, *The Structures of Nations and Empires* (New York: Charles Scribner's and Sons, 1959), 272.

25 Reinhold Niebuhr, *Moral Man and Immoral Society* (New York: Charles Scribner's and Sons, 1932), 4.

NOTES TO CHAPTER II

1 Hannah Arendt, "Thinking and Moral Considerations," *Social Research*, XXXVIII (Autumn, 1971), 417–46.
2 New York Times, January 4, 1977, p. 37.
3 Important Books by Reinhold Niebuhr include: *Moral Man and Immoral Society* (1932); *Christianity and Power Politics* (1940); *The Children of Light and the Children of Darkness* (1944); *Faith and History* (1949); *The Nature and Destiny of Man* (1949); *The Irony of American History* (1952); *Christian Realism and Political Problems* (1953); *The Self and the Dramas of History* (1955); *Pious and Secular America* (1958); *The Structures of Nations and Empires* (1959); *Love and Justice* (1967).
4 Reinhold Niebuhr, Sermon at Union Seminary, New York, delivered on May 10, 1960.
5 June Bingham, *Courage to Change* (New York: Charles Scribner's and Sons, 1961), 12.
6 Reinhold Niebuhr, "Human Nature and Social Change," *Christian Century*, (March, 1933), 363.
7 Reinhold Niebuhr, *The Irony of American History* (London: Nisbet and Co., 1952), 54.
8 Hans J. Morgenthau, *Politics Among Nations* (5th ed.; New York: Alfred A. Knopf, 1973), 27.
9 *Ibid.*, 34.
10 *Ibid.*, 189.
11 Roscoe Pound, *Philosophical Theory and International Law* (Leyden: Bibliotheca Visseriana, 1923), 74.
12 Morgenthau, *Politics Among Nations*, 196.
13 Arthur Schlesinger, Jr., *Early Writings, Walter Lippmann* (New York: Liveright, 1970), 71.
14 *Ibid.*, 88–89.
15 George F. Kennan, *American Diplomacy, 1900–1950* (Chicago: University of Chicago Press, 1951), 93.
16 George F. Kennan, "Foreign Policy and Christian Conscience," *Atlantic*, CCIII (May, 1959), 49.

NOTES TO CHAPTER III

1 Both Niebuhr's and Morgenthau's statements were quoted on the dust jacket of Mitrany's last summary volume, *The Functional Theory of Politics* (New York: St. Martin's Press, 1975).

NOTES TO CHAPTER IV

1 Tribute by the author to Agnes R. Thompson, August 25, 1976.
2 H. L. A. Fisher, *Political Prophecies* (Oxford: Clarendon Press, 1919), 4–8.
3 *Ibid.*
4 Kingman Brewster, "Remarks on the Uses of Knowledge and the Consequences of Knowing," *Vanderbilt University Centennial* (Nashville: Vanderbilt University, 1976), 46.

Notes

5 Louis J. Halle, "The Application of Morality to Foreign Policy" (MS presented at Department of State Conference on "Ethics and Foreign Policy," University of Virginia, June 13–15, 1977), 3.

6 *Ibid.*

7 Soedjatmoko, "Remarks," *Vanderbilt University Centennial* (Nashville: Vanderbilt University, 1976), 56–57.

8 *Ibid.*, 57–58.

9 *Ibid.*, 60.

10 *Ibid.*, 62–63.

11 Jonathan Swift, *Gulliver's Travels*, ed. Martin Price (New York: Bobbs-Merrill Co., 1963), 134.

12 R. Crawford Pratt, "Universities and Social Values in the Developing Areas: Some Reflections," in Kenneth W. Thompson, Barbara R. Fogel, and Helen E. Danner (eds.), *Higher Education for Social Change* (2 vols.; New York: Praeger Press, 1977), II, 530–34.

13 *The Speeches of the Right Honourable George Canning* (6 vols.; London: James Ridgway, 1845), VI, 109–12.

Index

Index

Index

Index

Index

Index

Truman, Harry S., 30, 43, 112
Tucker, Robert, 30

"Ugly American", 118
United Nations, 1, 5, 42, 67, 87, 126, 152
United Nations Educational, Scientific
  and Cultural Organization (UNESCO),
  62, 64, 65, 75
United States, 1, 14, 16, 22, 23, 54, 131
United States Assistance for Interna-
  tional Development (USAID), 62
Universalism, 80
Universities and values, 147–52
University of Chicago, 74
University of Dar es Salaam, 65, 144, 149,
  151
University of Ghana, 146
University of Ibadan, 144, 146, 149
University of Minnesota, 77
University of the Philippines, 83, 149
University of Science and Technology
  (Kumasi, Ghana), 63
Utopianism, 29, 32, 33, 34, 35, 64

Values: theories of, ix, 7–9, 106; crisis in,
  x, 1–9, 105; and their context, 7–8;
  competing and conflicting, 38; and
  education, 136–56; mentioned, 23, 38,
  49, 105, 106
Vance, Cyrus, 14, 45
Van Dusen, Henry Pitt, 137
Vanocur, Sander, 3
Vietnam War, 21, 41–42, 57, 106, 125

War, 20, 23
WASPS (White Anglo-Saxon Protestants),
  9
Wharton, Clifton R., 76
White, Gilbert, 39
Whitehead, Alfred North, 142
Wilhelm II, Kaiser, 16
Willits, Joseph H., 137
Wills, Gary, 9
Wilson, George Grafton, 35
Wilson, Woodrow, 15, 38, 40, 54, 55, 129,
  132, 154
Wisconsin University, 74–75
Weimar, Germany, 6
Wellhausen, Edwin, 102
Wordsworth, William, 121
World Bank, 6, 43, 62
World Environmental Conference, 1
World Food Conference, 1, 87, 88
World Food Council, 87, 88, 89, 90
World Health Organization (WHO), 102
World Population Conference, 1
World War II, 55
Wright, Quincy, 35

Yellow fever, 95
York, Herbert F., 112
Yugoslavia, 39

Zaire, 83
Zumwalt, Elmo, 40